The Power of Organizational Knowledge

Is knowledge powerful? Do leaders and those aspiring really understand the importance and power of organizational knowledge? Can knowing accelerate one's career journey, while not knowing disrupt success? Will leaders and organizations achieve their full potential and mission without leveraging organizational knowledge? This book is for leaders, aspiring leaders, professionals, students, performance improvement practitioners and strategists regardless of industry. It provides a quick, clear, and concise guide for readers to understand organizational knowledge, create knowledge transfer plans and leverage knowledge to lead from the front. Without knowledge, leaders and their organizations will eventually operationally perish.

In this book, leaders will learn the power of the following:

- Strategic knowledge
- Knowledge related to organizational governance and structure
- Creating knowledge plans and capturing and sharing knowledge
- Leveraging organizational knowledge in integrating organizations and building teams
- Knowledge in leadership decision making

The Power of Organizational Knowledge

11 Keys That Help Leaders Leverage Accurate Insight, Data, and Metrics

Casey J. Bedgood

Routledge
Taylor & Francis Group

A PRODUCTIVITY PRESS BOOK

First published 2023
by Routledge
605 Third Avenue, New York, NY 10158

and by Routledge
4 Park Square, Milton Park, Abingdon, Oxon, OX14 4RN

Routledge is an imprint of the Taylor & Francis Group, an informa business

ISBN: 978-1-032-32633-7 (hbk)
ISBN: 978-1-032-32631-3 (pbk)
ISBN: 978-1-003-31625-1 (ebk)

DOI: 10.4324/9781003316251

Typeset in Minion
by Apex CoVantage, LLC

Contents

Preface

The genesis of this book is many years of watching top leaders and their organizations struggle to reach their full potential. Years ago, a large service organization was conducting a national search for a new top leader. One candidate stood out from the rest of the pack. During the interview sessions with the governing board, the top leader asked for a current organizational chart of the enterprise.

Surprisingly, the governing body did not have one, because it did not exist. The governing body could only speak loosely about the organization's structure and nothing formal was on paper. The governing body's leaders eventually selected this visionary leader for the top leadership position. This leader was nationally renowned for thought leadership, showcased in many national keynote speeches, and possessed an uncanny amount of IQ and EQ (emotional intelligence).

The leader amassed a top leadership team of national experts with exceptional skills, IQ, EQ and track records of industry success. As time passed, the top leader's vision, strategy, and roadmap to make the enterprise a national leader hit constant potholes. After several years, the organization took an operational nosedive. Outcomes tied to value (i.e., service, cost, quality of services) continued to decline, and eventually, the leadership team was dispersed. Some made their way into retirement, while others transitioned to other organizations.

Looking back, the million-dollar question is, why did this visionary leader and their team fail? The leader was above average in the traditional skill sets for the industry. Their vision was also unprecedented. However, none of these attributes worked. Why?

After further consideration and analysis, the kryptonite was clear. The top leader and their team failed to properly assess, plan for, and mitigate organizational knowledge. What they did not know eventually destroyed their vision, plans, strategy, and career trajectory. As the adage goes, we don't know what we don't measure. What leaders don't know will eventually adversely impact them, their customers, and ultimately their organization.

Consequently, this book is being written to help leaders avoid the pitfalls of not knowing. Moreover, it will provide a simple road map to assist leaders in leveraging the power of organizational knowledge. Is knowledge powerful? In short, most leaders and governing bodies don't answer that question until it is too late. As Hosea (4:6, NIV) wrote, 'My people perish for a lack of knowledge.'

To reach one's full potential, knowledge must be harnessed, channeled, and magnified to ensure that pitfalls are avoided, and each step along the career journey is a tollgate leading to the operational promised land.

About the Author

Casey J. Bedgood is an author, a thought leader and a master change agent with over 20 years of healthcare leadership experience. He is the author of: *The Ride of a Lifetime, The Ideal Performance Improvement Eco System, The ABCs of Designing Performance Improvement Programs, Conquering the Giants, Fit for the Fight* and *The Mystery of Leadership*. He is a Six Sigma Black Belt and an accomplished author. Over the years, Casey's work has been recognized, sourced, and modeled by national and global best practice organizations in the healthcare industry and beyond. He has amassed a portfolio of dozens of publications on topics such as thought leadership, knowledge transfer, performance improvement, strategic design, innovative thinking, transformation and quality management systems (QMS). Subsequently, many large complex healthcare enterprises across the US, Canada, and Singapore have sourced and sought after Casey's thought leadership expertise.

Casey earned a BBA Magna Cum Laude from Mercer University and a Master of public administration from Georgia College & State University (GCSU). He is an IISE Lean Green Belt, Six Sigma Green Belt and Six Sigma Black Belt. He has also been CAP trained via GE and he is a member of the American College of Healthcare Executives (ACHE).

Introduction

Is all knowledge the same? Is ignorance bliss or does knowledge really make a difference? Will knowledge transfer itself or is help needed? Do all leaders really understand the concept of knowledge transfer? Will organizational knowledge determine whether or not an organization succeeds in the long term? Will a lack of knowledge prevent leaders and organizations from reaching their full potential and fulfilling their mission? Is knowledge easily transferrable or is a plan required? Is it possible to harness organizational knowledge and leverage it to achieve optimal success? We will answer these and many other questions in the following chapters.

This book is being written for leaders, aspiring leaders, professionals, students, performance improvement practitioners and strategists across industries. The purpose is to provide a clear and concise guide for readers to understand organizational knowledge, create knowledge transfer plans, and leverage knowledge to lead from the front.

In *The Power of Organizational Knowledge: 11 Keys That Help Leaders Leverage Accurate Insight, Data, and Metrics*, readers will learn many topics including—but not limited to—the power of strategic knowledge, the power of knowledge related to organizational governance and structure, the power of knowledge plans, the power of capturing and sharing knowledge, the power of leveraging organizational knowledge in integrating organizations and building teams, and the power of knowledge in leadership decision making.

The reality is simple. Knowledge matters. It is an essential component for leaders, their teams, and their organizations at large to succeed in the long term. What we don't know can and will be a problem at some point along the career journey. The more we know, the better off we are. Thus, leaders and their organizations must realize, value, and leverage the power of organizational knowledge. Otherwise, they will simply die on the vine (operationally speaking) due to a lack of knowing, insight, and forethought.

1

The Power of Strategic Knowledge

The purpose of this chapter is to provide a simple, realistic and real-world overview of strategic planning. It is amazing how many thought leaders don't have a basic planning process that is effective. Moreover, it is often shocking, how many organizations have a strategic planning process but don't know if it is successful. Simply put, a process may exist, but it fails to move the organization forward and no one can explain why.

The genesis of this chapter is a compilation of many conversations over the years with senior leadership teams in the service industry. Most were struggling with operational outcomes and pursued a siloed approach to make the organization perform better. Unfortunately, many failed to improve due to a lack of knowledge.

1.1 MEASURES OF SUCCESS

When planning strategically, the number one question to ask is, 'How do you know your strategic planning process is successful?' Often, leaders will respond with a mirage of perspectives: We know our planning process is successful because we have a process. We are successful at planning strategically because our process occurs each year at the same time. Our strategy process is successful because we conduct a market assessment each year and understand market gaps. Does this really mean the organization is successful in strategic planning? The short answer is arguably not.

There are several object measures of a successful strategic planning process. The first step to success is having a process. The process should be formalized and consistent and should occur each year. Preferably, the strategic planning process should occur the same time each year so the enterprise establishes a cadence that becomes part of the operating norms and culture.

The second indicator of a successful strategy process is ensuring that the process is anchored in the organization's vision, mission and value statements. The vision is simply where the organization is headed or desires to go. The mission outlines why the organization exists. The organization's values are guardrails of expected behavior selected by top leaders and the governing body.

An offshoot of values often overlooked is norms. Operating norms are what actually happens in the organization's work areas. A pitfall that leaders must avoid in strategic planning is ensuring that values (what is written on the wall) align with norms (what happens in the work areas). If not, a crisis and operational chaos will follow. Does the adage, 'do as I say not as I do' ring a bell?

The third indicator of strategy planning success is to have the annual process on the organization's operating calendar. An operating calendar is simply a showcase outlining the major events or focal points for leaders throughout the course of the year. Typically, items may include, but not be limited to, budgets, goal setting, staff and leader performance evaluations and the like. The goal is to include a finite or limited number of big-ticket items that leaders must have on their radar each month so they don't get lost in other operational priorities. The key is, for leaders, to ensure that the strategic planning process is an organizational priority that everyone can speak to. If leaders cannot speak to the process, then more than likely it will not be successful.

The fourth litmus test for strategic planning is standardization. The question to answer is simple. Is the process the same for everyone? Everyone implies all business units regardless of size, scope or complexity.

In a recent engagement, a thought leader was assigned the task of assessing a large service organization's strategic planning process. The organization was spread over a large geographic area with many thousands of staff and leaders. There were many business units represented ranging from hundreds of leaders and staff to thousands. The scope, complexity and reach of services also varied greatly.

In the initial conversations with large business unit leaders, the thought leader simply asked one question. Can you show me your strategic planning process in 15 slides or less? Only a couple of the leaders had a semi-formal process. However, they were different. Moreover, the other business unit leaders did not have a standardized strategic planning process. Immediately, the thought leader realized that strategic planning was not present, effective or standardize. Thus, it was not successful. No further assessment was warranted.

The key to passing this litmus test is to ensure that the process is standardized across the board. All leaders should have a cyclical process where they use the same templates and guiding principles. As important, each leader should be able to explain the process and their contributions to the process. Otherwise, variation will run ramped and derail the organization's strategy.

The fifth measure of success for strategic planning is who the process involves. Are all relevant stakeholders involved? Is strategic planning only reserved for the organization's top leaders? Are the plan and its expected end shared with the entire organization including front-line staff members? If not, the plan is not a success.

An effective strategy process should include all relevant stakeholders. These stakeholders range from the governing body to the front-line staff. Everyone should be a part of the process in some way. If not, the organization's strategic plan will be minimally effective.

Finally, the ultimate measure of success for strategy planning is its links. Does the plan link gaps and goals? Does the plan link budgets to goals? Does the plan link goals to outcomes?

In short, there are four global links for a successful strategic planning process. First, the process must link gaps to goals. The premise is simple. Leaders should set goals to fill the organization's operational gaps. Next, the process must link goals to budgets. How will an organization be successful if it sets arbitrary budgets not tied to targets? In short, it will not.

The premise is to set budgets that ensure that resources are available to meet goals. This is one of the biggest pitfalls organizations succumb to in the planning process. Next, leaders must link the first three links to organizational outcomes. If the organization fails to meet its expected goals, then the first three links must be reassessed and corrected. Otherwise, the process is a very expensive waste of time, resources and organizational focus.

Let's take a practical look at a real-world example. A thought leader was engaged to help a top leadership team turn around a large service organization. The organization struggled for several years with customer satisfaction, costs and quality of services provided. As time passed, the outcomes worsened. The impact on the bottom line was in the tens of millions of dollars unfavorably.

The organization had a fragmented strategic planning process that occurred most years at the same time. Some leaders could speak to the process, while others could not. Each year the budget process took priority over all other operational calendar priorities. Simply put, the organization viewed its success as measured by having a rigid budget process even if it was not tied to goals or gaps. The profit margin was more important, obviously, than the other links.

In retrospect, the thought leader discovered that the organization's top leaders were not aware of current and expected operational gaps. A micro-example was related to improvement resources. The organization identified several high-profile opportunities worth over $100 million in waste. However, no resources were budgeted to train, staff or deployed talent to eliminate these wasteful occurrences. Thus, the organization's avoidable costs continued to grow at astronomical rates.

As noted, we can't fix what we don't break. The takeaway and ultimate test of a strategic planning process are whether or not the process produces the expected end. Are gaps, goals, budgets and outcomes linked? If not, the process is not a success and must be reengineered. Otherwise, the organization is conducting a test of futility that will never hit the target.

1.2 STRATEGIC PLANNING PROCESS

1.2.1 Gap Analysis

The first step of the strategic planning process should include the gap analysis. Here, leaders and their organizations will focus on both internal and external gaps. External gaps pertain to those that exist outside the organization. The main focus here would be on the market(s), communities and customer bases served by the organization.

Let's use a healthcare example to explain the context. Annually, top-performing hospitals and health systems complete a community health-needs assessment that provides an overview of the communities served.

Specifically, this assessment helps leaders understand their customer base better. Common focal points may include, but are not limited to, poverty rates by zip code, access to housing, access to healthcare, insurance coverage, assess to food or technology and the like. The identified gaps are leveraged as strategic priorities to ensure that the organization is providing the healthcare needs of the communities.

Another external gap analysis example would be a review of market and/or industry service line data. Here, healthcare leaders leverage data and analytics to assess which service lines will grow, remain flat or decline over the next three to ten years. Practical service lines may include emergency care, children's care, women's services, surgical services and many others. The key here is for leaders to know which type of business they should be in and what service lines will be successful for a long term.

It is important to note that industry and market data may vary. The healthcare industry in the US, for example, may forecast that emergency-care demand declines across the country. However, some geographic markets may see increases in the demand for these services based on the population and customer bases. Irrespectively, external gaps must be identified and incorporated into the strategic planning process.

In contrast to external gaps, organizations must also consider internal strategic gaps. Here, leaders should focus on items such as people, service, cost, revenue and quality of services as a start. Common people or talent KPIs (key performance indicators) may include vacancy rates, turnover rates, days to onboard new talent, employee engagement scores and the like.

Service scores typically include customer satisfaction rates. In healthcare, for example, top leaders take great interest in rating such as overall satisfaction, likely to recommend to others. The key is to determine what the organization is doing well to satisfy its customers and where the gaps are located.

The financials are an obvious and often highest priority for top leaders. Here, the organization reviews historical and current financial data. The most important question often posed is, 'Are we making money and will we do so in the future.' The goal is to look at trends over time. Ideally, revenues would increase year by year, while costs decrease. Thus, margins would be healthy. In today's world, this is not always the case. Thus, leaders must know where their financial gaps are or are expected to be in the future so planning is sufficient.

Quality is also a common target in strategic planning. Quality may mean different things in different industries. In healthcare, quality may be represented by infection rates, fall, harm, employee injuries and the like. In manufacturing, quality may be directly tied to metrics around defects in producing widgets, for example. Irrespective of foci, quality matters and determines the value each customer receives from the company. Thus, leaders must know their quality strengths and where the cost of poor-quality lies.

The main focus is to determine whether the organization historically has met goals tied to these value streams or not. There are three basic questions to ask:

- Are we meeting goal?
- Are we improving to achieve goal?
- Is our performance in or out of control?

A simple run chart and control chart would be prime tools to display these data. However, the takeaway is that leaders should understand the organization's internal gaps so corrections can be planned for in the strategy process. Otherwise, it is just planning for the sake of planning.

1.2.2 Planning

The second part of the strategic planning process is planning. Once internal and external gaps are identified, leaders work to establish goals for the present and future. The intent of goals is to fill the gaps. Typically, a five-year plan is the normal forecasted timeframe for all service lines, value streams and plans. Goals tied to the KPIs previously noted, such as revenues, cost, quality and people, are always a high priority. The key here is for leaders to ensure that goals are realistic, resourced, measurable and tied to industry's best practice benchmarks.

If 'softball' goals are set for strategic goals, then the organization will not make much forward progress. The adage of 'what sparkles doesn't always shine' applies here. Although the organization meets these goals, it doesn't really mean much. In contrast, if goal setting is unrealistic or overly aggressive, leaders will have little to no chance of meeting the goals. Thus, team building, synergy and morale will decline. The end result will be long-term organizational failure.

The macro-perspective of planning also involves creating sub-plans. Here, leaders focus on important areas that are required for organizational success in the long term. Typically, leaders may focus on talent plans, for example. The goal is to ensure that the organization has the human resources needed to meet current and future customer expectations.

Leaders often include capital plans into the process. These financial plans include large dollar purchases of single items typically. The qualifying dollar amount for this category of expenditure is organization dependent. In healthcare, for example, an X-ray machine that costs over $1 million is a good example of a capital item. The purchase of an ambulance of over $100,000 is another capital example.

Other strategic plans may include infrastructure (new buildings), technology, continuous improvement and the like. Irrespective of type, strategic plans and their offshoots should focus on items, services or playbooks crucial to the organization's viability, growth and long-term market relevance.

1.2.3 Implementation

The next step in the strategic planning process is implementation. Once all the goals, plans and playbooks are configured to fill gaps, the plans are implemented across the enterprise. The key here is that the whole organization has a role to play. Thus, it is imperative that all relevant stakeholders are involved in the strategy process as appropriate, understand the goals and actively participate. The biggest pitfall in strategy implementation is a siloed approach where only the few are involved or participate.

Think of a baseball game where only two players take the field during the world series. The gaps in the field from missing players form easy targets for the opposing team. Thus, an impossible win–lose scenario for the team is created where the probability of success is near zero. The goal here is for the enterprise to achieve synergies by working in unison. A synergy is 'increased effectiveness that results when two or more people or businesses work together' (Merriam-Webster, 2022).

The keys to success for strategic plan implementation are as follows:

1. Everyone knows the plan, process and their role.
2. Everyone contributes to success.
3. Everyone contributes to excellence.

4. Everyone has a safe place to succeed or fail with the expectation to try again if failure results.
5. Wins are celebrated by top leadership and the governing body.
6. Communication of the plan, process and progress is regular and reaches all stakeholders.

1.2.4 Reassessment

Once strategic plans are created to fill gaps and implemented, they must be reassessed frequently. The key term here is frequency. How often organizations review the progress of strategic plan outcomes varies. However, the general rule of thumb in today's world is sooner is better than later.

The key for reassessing strategic plans successfully is measurement. Leaders don't know what they don't measure. Ignorance is never bliss. Thus, progress to goals must be measured frequently. Some organizations review their progress weekly, some monthly, some quarterly and others annually. The key is to fit the reassessment plan with the industry, organizational needs and overarching strategic plan.

When reassessing progress of strategic plans, often leaders focus on several attributes. Are we meeting base goals tied to key anchors such as service, cost, revenue and quality? If so, are we meeting stretch goals tied to each anchor? Has goal attainment been validated externally to the process owner, which adds validity to the measure? For example, if a leader espouses that their division met its base and stretch goals for revenue for the quarter, has the finance leader validated this assertion objectively? If progress to goal is lacking, the organization should reassess and pivot quickly.

Leaders also often reassess or remeasure market drivers or disruptors. If strategic plans were based off of market or industry data and the forecasts change mid-year, leaders should pivot their plans to ensure proper alignment. There is nothing worse strategically than charting an operational course and staying the course when viable targets have shifted position. The chance of success in this case is near zero.

The takeaway is that reassessment is a constant process. The market and customer expectations are always changing. As change grows, so does the risk to the organization if not planned properly. The rate and speed of strategic reassessments and pivots are dependent upon market drivers, customer bases and organizational priorities.

1.3 STRATEGIC PLANNING TEMPLATES

1.3.1 Timeline and Tollgates

As leaders and their organizations plan strategically, it is often helpful to use a macro-timeline and tollgate template as noted in Figure 1.1. Here, leaders map out their journey usually with just a few high-level steps for the process to be successful. Also, corresponding completion dates are noted per tollgate so the organization stays on track during the process.

As noted in Figure 1.1, the organization plans the assessment and gap analysis for a specific time period. Once complete, the planning phase begins and lasts for a specified time period. Then, the plans, playbooks and goals are implemented. After implementation, the reassessment occurs with results being reported up to senior leadership and the governing body. Finally, pivots or adjustments are made as new gaps arise. The key is that the process is cyclical with a start, end and measurable tollgates along the way.

1.3.2 SWOT Analysis

A SWOT analysis is one of the best battle test tools to use during an assessment. For this conversation, as noted in Figure 1.2, the template has four parts.

The focal points are strategy, operations, people and regulatory—the S standards for strengths. Here, leaders look for internal strengths of the organization. Common examples may include strong profit margin, low infection rates, low turnover rates, declining operational costs, high employee engagement and the like. The key is for leaders and other stakeholders to assess and collectively create an exhaustive list of the organization's internal strengths.

FIGURE 1.1
Timelines and tollgates Macro-View.

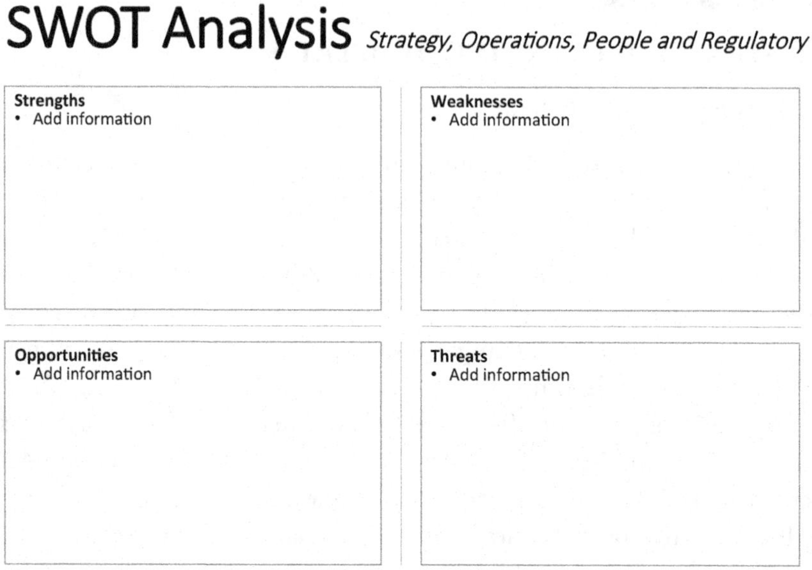

SWOT Analysis Strategy, Operations, People and Regulatory

Strengths	Weaknesses
• Add information	• Add information

Opportunities	Threats
• Add information	• Add information

FIGURE 1.2

Source: IISE Lean Green Belt (2016)

The W stands for internal weaknesses. Here, leaders and stakeholders work together to compile an exhaustive list of the organization's internal weaknesses. Common examples may include declining revenue streams, less than expected customer satisfaction rates, cost of poor quality and many others too numerous to mention. The key is for the organization to identify both obvious and hidden weaknesses. Thus, a comprehensive and multi dimensional team of stakeholders is needed for this assessment to gain the clearest picture of the organization's internal weaknesses.

The O stands for external opportunities. Here, leaders and stakeholders work collectively to identify perceived and actual opportunities for the organization to improve. Common findings may include market growth for expanded business in a neighboring service area, training opportunities via partnership with a regional training institute, potential joint venture with a local competitor to globally provide cheaper, safer and more accessible health services and many others. The key is for stakeholders to create an exhaustive list of actual and perceived opportunities. The adage of 'leave no stone unturned' applies here.

The T stands for threats. Leaders and stakeholders work diligently to identify any external threats to the organization. Examples may include the entrance of a competitor or rival into the organization's primary service area, new regulatory requirements that increase operational costs by 10%, local competitor offering salaries 20% higher for certain skill sets and others. The key is for leaders to quickly and regularly identify, assess and mitigate threats to the organization's market position.

1.3.3 Gap Analysis

As noted in Figure 1.3, a gap analysis template is a good tool for the strategic planning gap analysis process. This tool, in its most basic form, has four columns as noted in the figure—the identified gap, the scope, the risk level and the owner. The overarching foci are service, cost, quality, people and regulatory attributes that may pose a gap to the organization's forward progress.

The most important aspect of this tool is the risk column. Risk is calculated as high, medium or low. As the legend details, high-risk attributes are immediate jeopardy to life and safety. Medium risk indicates that the attribute is a risk to the organization's mission. Low risk is an important item, but it is not critical to the organization fulfilling its mission.

Gap	Scope (Department; Entity; System)	Risk (High/Medium/Low)	Owner

- High Risk: Immediate Jeopardy to Life and Safety
- Medium Risk: Critical to Mission
- Low Risk: Important, but not Critical to Mission

FIGURE 1.3

Gap analysis—service, cost, quality, people, and regulatory.

Let's take a practical look at the tool using a healthcare example. Hospital A has low-quality scores tied to higher-than-average infection rates for surgical patients and higher than industry average operating costs. The gaps are infections and costs. Both attributes' scopes relate to the hospital in question. The infection rates are of high risk as they are an immediate threat to life and safety. In contrast, the operational cost issues are of medium risk, as they don't directly impact life and safety. However, they affect the hospital's mission. Irrespectively, both costs and infections are a high priority for leaders and should be assigned to an owner for resolution.

The takeaway is that the gap analysis tool is helpful for leaders to identify, assess and prioritize strategic gaps that will impede the organization's forward progress. The key is for leaders to systematically address gaps instead of trying to boil the ocean in addressing everything at once. Success will come from prioritizing risks and applying resources to the highest threats first.

1.3.4 Service Line Risk Assessment Tool

Figure 1.4 outlines a risk assessment for service in health as an example.

This is a value tool during the planning phase of the strategic process. Here, leaders list current and new services in consideration. There are three attributes of focus for each service: profitability, growth and current volume trend. The cumulative measure is assigned a risk score and eventual risk level. The goal is for leaders to assess these services, identify the highest risk options and avoid them by selecting low-risk services.

As noted in the figure, there are three services being risk assessed: labs, diagnostics and surgery. The laboratory offerings are profitable with

Service	Profitable? 1-Yes 2-No	Growth? 1-Yes 2-No	Current Volume Trend 1-Increasing 2-Flat 3-Declining	Risk Score Add Columns 2– 4 *Lower Score = Lower Risk	Risk Level • High (Risk Score > 5) • Avg (Risk Score = 5) • Low (Risk Score < 5)
Labs	1	2	1	4	Low Risk
Diagnostics	2	2	3	7	High Risk
Surgery	1	1	3	5	Avg Risk

FIGURE 1.4

Risk assessment: services.

limited market growth outside the organization's primary service area. Also, the current demand for this service is increasing in the market. Thus, it is of low risk and a good fit for the strategic plan playbook.

In contrast, diagnostics such as imaging, X-rays and CAT scans (CT) are of high risk. They are not profitable, have little growth potential outside the primary service area and the current demand for those services is declining. Thus, the leaders should consider not including these services in the playbook or at most limiting them.

The middle-of-the-road service is surgery. This is an average-risk proposition. The surgery service line is profitable with growth potential outside the primary service area of the organization. However, current demand inside the market is declining and, thus, it is of average risk. Therefore, leaders must plan wisely and find innovative ways to extend the service to other markets so growth and demand increase.

The takeaway from the figure is that it's a simple and basic tool for strategic planning. Leaders can modify the tool for the specific industry and organizational playbook. All organizations have service lines of some fashion. However, the million-dollar question to be answered is, does the organization know which services are of high, medium or low risk? In layman's terms, what services should be included or excluded in the organization's playbook using a methodology instead of perception? This tool is a good conversation starter.

1.3.5 Five-Year Plan Template

As noted in Figure 1.5, another helpful strategic planning tool is the five-year plan template.

Here, leaders identify focus areas. As noted in the figure, common foci are service, financials, quality and people. This is a healthcare example, but the tool can be modified for any industry.

Next, leaders forecast goals for the next five years (by year) for each focus area. Goals will vary based on industry along with scope, size and complexity of the organization. The takeaway is for leaders to forecast realistic, measurable and industry-benchmarked goals that add value to the organization's strategic plan. One important piece of the template is the strategic theme row. Here, leaders identify a strategic theme for each year. The goals coincide with each strategic theme to ensure that the organization makes forward progress.

Focus Area	Year 1	Year 2	Year 3	Year 4	Year 5
Strategic Theme	*Foundation*	*Transform Culture*	*High Performance*	*Magnify Wins*	*Standardize*
Service (Customer Satisfaction)	• 80% Satisfied				
Financial • Revenue • Costs • Capital	• $3 million • $2 million • $1 million				
Quality and Safety • Mortality • Infections	• 50th Percentile • 50th Percentile				
People • Engagement • Employee Satisfaction • Turnover	• < 15%				

FIGURE 1.5
Five-year plan template.

Let's take a practical look at the template. As noted, the view or forecast is for five years. The strategic theme for year 1 is foundation. The leaders are using this as a starting point or foundation for the strategic direction of the organization.

The focus areas are service, financials, quality and people. Each individual focal point has a specific goal for year 1. Leaders would need to map this process out over the next four years to complete the template. For service, the organization's ideal goal is for 80% of its customers to be satisfied with its services. The quality scores are benchmarked off the 50th percentile for the industry. This means that, if the organization meets the goal, they are as good in these focus areas as half the country. Moreover, the goal for employee turnover in year 1 is less than 15%.

The takeaway is that the tool forces leaders and the governing body to look ahead and plan accordingly. This tool can be used at any organizational level including top leadership, divisional or on the front lines for strategic planning. It is imperative to note that, if leader uses this concept or one similar to this concept, the template is identical for all levels so all leaders are singing from the same sheet of music.

1.3.6 Operational Calendar Template

Figure 1.6 outlines a simple operational calendar with a few real-world examples as a conversation starter. The key here is for leaders to create a simple calendar representing the operating year for their organization.

In the figure, the focus areas include budgets, goal setting, strategic planning, employee performance evaluations, employee engagement surveys and governing body meetings.

It's imperative to note that, regardless of focus area, their timing is of utmost importance. As noted previously, leaders cannot put the cart before the horse during planning. If budgets are scheduled before goals are set, for example, then the organization may not have the resources needed to meet its goals for the year. If organizational goal setting occurs before the strategic gap analysis process, then goals may not fill the realized gaps. Leaders should plan the calendar for their organization with consideration for sequence and flow of the strategic process.

The key here is for leaders to use a simple template that is accurate, aligns with the organization's processes and is relatable to all leaders and staff. Anyone should be able to view the operational calendar at a glance and discern progress to date along with what is coming next. The pearl is simplicity.

1.3.7 Communication Template

One of the most important aspects of strategic planning is communicating the vision, plan and road ahead. A simple communication template as noted in Figure 1.7 is a good example of how leaders can forecast the communication campaign. The measure of success for any communication is to ensure that the target audience is reached, the message is received and all stakeholders understand their role in the strategic planning process.

Focus Area	Jan	Feb	Mar	Apr	May	Jun	July	Aug	Sep	Oct	Nov	Dec
Budgets						X						
Goal Setting				X								
Strategic Planning	X											
Employee Evaluations								X				
Employee Engagement Surveys									X			
Governing Body Meetings	X	X	X	X	X	X	X	X	X	X	X	X

FIGURE 1.6
Operational calendar entity view.

Mode	Target Audience	Frequency	Measure of Success?
Executive Leadership Meetings	Executives	Add info	Add info
Program Leadership Meetings	Program Leaders	Add info	Add info
Market Leadership Meetings	Market Leaders		
Newsletter	All staff and leaders		
E-mails			
Social Media			
Staff Meetings			
Integration Team Meetings			

FIGURE 1.7
Communication template.

As noted in the figure, there are four columns: mode, target audience, frequency and measure of success. The communication mode simply entails the method in which communication will occur. As noted, the template includes e-mails, newsletters, social media posts, leadership meetings and team meetings with staff. These are just abstract examples for the purpose of this conversation.

The target audience is also very important. Who is intended to receive the communication? The audience should be tailored for each communication. Some audiences may include senior leaders, department leaders, program leaders and even all staff. The goal is to ensure that the organization avoids leaving anyone behind during the journey.

Frequency of communication is another important attribute worth noting. Some communications require daily updates to top leaders, while others may be monthly or quarterly. The risk level of the initiative will correlate with the communication frequency. The higher the risk, importance or threat, the more frequent communications are required.

The final attribute in Figure 1.7 is a measure of success. As noted, no one wants to talk or message themselves needlessly. Thus, communication leaders need to ensure that there is a tangible means of measuring the success of communications. If an e-mail is sent to 1,000 leaders, tracking read notices per leader may be a viable source. For social media, posts to the enterprise, usage rates or response counts may also work. The point is for leaders to know what modes of communication work for their populations and ensure that the message is received by intended stakeholders.

1.3.8 Reassessment Timeline Template

As leaders begin the reassessment step of the strategic planning process, it's a good rule of thumb to map out a macro-timeline with tollgates. As noted in Figure 1.8, this is a monthly view. Some leaders may need a daily or weekly view for some initiatives. For this example, each month leaders should track identified gaps during scheduled strategic plan reassessments. For each gap, a mitigation plan is recommended. Simply put, what will be done to resolve the gap? Who owns the mitigation plan and was the gap resolved? Unresolved gaps should be escalated to top leadership and the governing body as needed.

The takeaway is for leaders to synthesize their reassessment efforts in a one-page document if possible. Then, socialize the list, progress and unresolved gaps frequently to all stakeholders for quick resolution.

1.3.9 Lessons Learned Template

At the end of the strategic planning process, it's imperative for leaders to conduct an after-action report of sorts. Also, strategic planning never really ends so this 'look back' is a continuous part of the process that

Month	Identified Gap(s)	Mitigation Plan	Owner	Gap Resolved? (Yes/No)
Jan				
Feb				
Mar				
Apr				
May				
Jun				
Jul				
Aug				
Sep				
Oct				
Nov				
Dec				

FIGURE 1.8
Reassessment timeline monthly.

should occur often. As noted in Figure 1.9, the lessons learned template can be simple or modified for complexity as needed.

There are a few simple considerations leaders should entertain. First, what worked with the previous strategic planning cycle? Second, what did not work? Third, what's the plan for those attributes that did not work during gap analysis, planning and implementation of the strategic plan? Finally, who owns the plan of correction?

The key here is for leaders to use the tool for a few purposes. First is to use the tool to celebrate wins and success stories. Leaders and teams should be recognized and praised for any positive wins along the strategic journey. Second, in the spirit of continuous improvement, leaders should always look for the next opportunity that will make the process better. This tool is a simple scoping document to bolster the continuous improvement pipeline. Third, leaders can use the template to track progress for corrections. More detail can be captured in different venues. However, the takeaway is to praise what worked, correct what did not work and track corrections to ensure that they are sustained for a long term.

What Worked?	What Didn't Work?	Plan for What Didn't Work	Owner

FIGURE 1.9
Lessons learned.

2

The Power of Governance Knowledge

The purpose of this chapter is to provide a very simple and concise framework for creating, cultivating and showcasing an organization's governance model. The genesis for this topic was noted in the forethought and introduction sections. Over the years, during many conversations with leaders at all levels its surprising how many cannot speak to their organization's governance structure. In some instances, leaders would not be able to draw or describe the organizational chart if they had to.

Again, everything is relative. Governance models range from simplistic to overly complicated based on the organization's size, scope and complexity. However, as with strategic knowledge, there is a litmus test here as well. The test for governance knowledge is simple:

- Is there a governance model in place?
- Is there a governance model showcase? (Preferably a one-page example of the governance structure.)
- Can leaders and staff speak accurately to the governance model structure, its functions, its reporting channels and the like?

If leaders and staff at all levels cannot speak to the organization's structure accurately, then obvious knowledge gaps exist.

By definition, governance is 'The act or process of governing or overseeing the control and direction of something (such as a country or an organization)' (Merriam-Webster, 2022). This concept is synonymous with authority, control, administration and oversight (Merriam-Webster, 2022). In layman's terms, governance of any organization simply relates to how the enterprise is structured and what accountability mechanisms exist to ensure what is supposed to happen actually occurs.

DOI: 10.4324/9781003316251-2

Governance functions include attributes such as meetings, review of documents, decision making, strategic planning, approvals, selection of top organizational leaders and many others too numerous to cover here. Ultimately, the governing body is responsible for the success or failure of the organization.

From a basic perspective, governance represents the operating structure or guardrails that keep the organization on track. Moreover, governance functions and associated leadership attributes ensure the organization's stability, success and long-term relevancy. As some of us learned years ago in Lean training, there is a formula for success for implementing change and driving ideal performance (IISE Lean Green Belt, 2016).

This formula encompasses contributing factors such as leadership, vision, a plan, people and resourcing, all of which are a by-product in some way of the governance model. For organizations to perform as intended, there must first be a vision. The vision simply outlines where the organization is headed. It's a future look over the horizon at the desired tollgates of the path ahead.

Second, leadership is also a critical component to success. Without leadership, there will be fear and anxiety. Often during leadership gaps, people ask the following:

- Who is responsible for 'x, y or z'?
- To whom do we go for help?
- Who do I report to?
- Who will complete my performance evaluation?

When these questions begin to swirl, it's a bad sign of a leadership gap and lack of knowledge.

Third, ideal performance is predicated on people. People are the most valuable resource to any organization. They also are the bearers of organizational culture or the way work gets done. Without people and cultural alignment, change or basic operations will miss the target. Simply put, if people are not aligned or don't understand the governance model, there will be little to no change or forward progress. The adage of 'pulling teeth' to get these done applies here.

The final components of driving ideal performance are a plan and associated resourcing. A lack of both attributes will produce false starts and frustration from stakeholders. The key is that knowledge of the organization's governance structure is powerful. When leaders, staff and other stakeholders understand how the organization is structured, who is responsible for what and to whom to go for help, success is much easier. In contrast, when this knowledge is lacking, the organization will struggle to produce outcomes, experience critical knowledge gaps and eventually fail.

2.1 SAMPLE GOVERNANCE STRUCTURES

In the following, we will briefly discuss basic examples of a sample organization's governance structure. It's important to note that these are only basic examples. Governance structures depend directly on the size, scope and complexity of the enterprise. Various industries and organizational types may have different structures.

2.1.1 Governance Model

In simplest terms, there are two focal points: the governance model and the organizational chart. As noted in Figure 2.1, a basic governance model has three layers. The first layer represents the strategic functions of the enterprise. Here, leaders and governing body members focus on the top priorities of the organization.

As noted in the figure, the governing body consists of multiple boards. The system board is ultimately responsible for all organization activity, success and failure. The market board for this respective geographic location reports up to the system board. Reporting up to the market board are the President's Council, subcommittees of the market board and other smaller boards representing small entities in the market.

The President's Council in this example is comprised of executive leaders for the market. In healthcare, for example, this council may be comprised of the CEO and other top leaders representing operations, strategy, finance, clinical operations, information technology and the like. The key is for the organization's top leaders to meet regularly, plan, strategize and execute the organization's priorities.

The subcommittees of the market board focus on operational issues that affect the organization's success in the long term. Here, leaders of specific specialties meet with board members on a regular basis to discuss issues, solve problems, approve items and plan for the future. In this example, subcommittees represent finance, technology, human resources and strategy. However, there are many other options here for membership and representation based on the organization's size, scope and complexity.

The local facility boards represent smaller facilities. These facilities in a healthcare setting, for example, may include smaller hospitals or entities with 100 or fewer employees. Also, they may represent small geographic regions such as one county. The key is for the smaller facilities to be represented to the market board and ultimately the system board.

The second layer of the draft governance model in Figure 2.1 relates to operational. Here, operational planning occurs. The steering committee for operations reports up to the President's council. This group of leaders represent, in this example, various tactical subcommittees related to strategy, operations, planning and other work streams. The work streams represent focal points that are pertinent to the organization's success, viability and long-term relevancy. Sample healthcare work streams in healthcare may include infection rates, continuous improvement, integration, synergy, knowledge transfer, standardization and many others.

The takeaway from Figure 2.1 is that leaders should create, cultivate and socialize the organization's governance model in one slide if possible. In this format, simple is better. The key is for leaders and staff (as appropriate) to be able to speak to, accurately describe and understand how the organization is structured. If they can answer the basics: How is the organization structured? Who is responsible for what? Can you describe the organization's governance structure? Then, there is a sense of knowing. If not, knowledge gaps exist.

2.1.2 Organizational Chart

An organizational chart is simply a showcase of the organization's reporting structure. We will briefly discuss three basic levels of organization structure: organizational view, division view and departmental view. This premise is simple. Leaders should capture reporting structures from front lines to the executive team. Again, it is imperative to note that organizational charts will vary based on the size, scope and

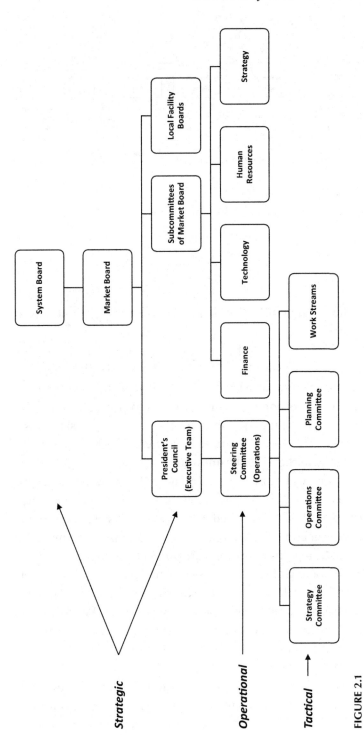

FIGURE 2.1
Governance model sample.

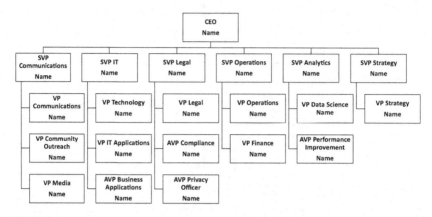

FIGURE 2.2
Organizational chart sample (organizational view).

complexity of the organization. The following are basic examples as a conversation starter.

In Figure 2.2, the focus is on the top leadership structure. Here, the reporting structure begins with the CEO. The CEO has six direct reporting senior vice presidents (i.e., SVPs). Each SVP represents a different function ranging from corporate communications to strategy. Each SVP has a host of direct reports ranging from vice presidents (i.e., VPs) to assistant vice presidents (i.e., AVPs). Again, each of these direct reports has a specialty tied directly to the SVP's business unit.

The basics are as follows. Ensure that the top layers of organizational leadership are represented on the chart. Include the official job title and name for each leader. In this example, the chart included three to four layers of leaders. Some organizations may be able to fit more layers in the chart, while others may not. Finally, ensure that the reporting structures are correct for each leader.

In Figure 2.3, the focus shifts to the division view. Here, a division leader (i.e., VP) is the group leader of operations, for example. The VP has an administrative assistant directly assigned to them. Four AVPs directly report to the vice president. Each AVP has a host of directors with various specialties that report to them. The key from this view is that the chart represents a division or a group.

As noted in Figure 2.2, the basics are simple and the same. Ensure that all leaders in the group are represented. Include a name for each leader. Some organizations also add a picture for each leader, but that's nice to

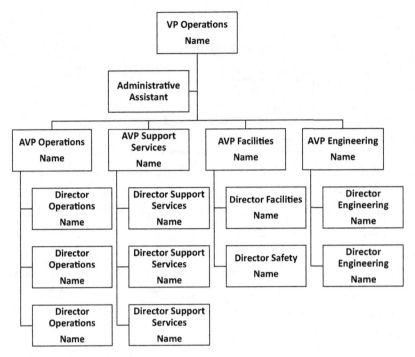

FIGURE 2.3
Organizational chart sample (divisional view).

have. Ensure that the reporting structure and alignment for each leader are accurate. The goal is to capture all reporting structures for the group in one chart that is easily and clearly displayed.

In Figure 2.4, this is a departmental view. The key is further down on the organizational chart we go, the more detail is needed. Here, the department is led by a director. The director also has a direct report administrative assistant. There are four other managers that directly report to the director. Each manager is represented by different geographic sites or locations. Each manager has two direct report supervisors that work either day or night. The front-line staff would report directly to the supervisors.

As with the other organizational charts, the basics are the same. Leaders should make sure that each leader is represented on the chart. The reporting alignments should represent accurate reporting structures. It's a good idea to include a name for each leader. A photo is optional, but not a bad idea if feasible.

In summary, knowledge pertaining to an organization's governance and structure is powerful. If leaders and staff don't know how the organization is

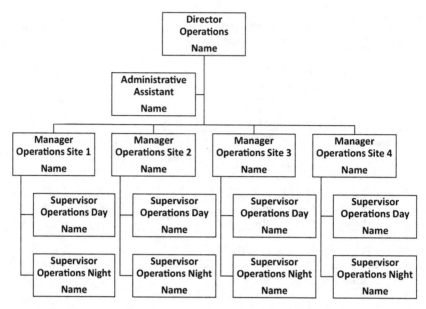

FIGURE 2.4

Organizational chart sample (departmental view).

structured, who they report to and who is responsible for what, then chaos, confusion and false starts will be commonplace. Moreover, if the organization does not have a simple governance model that can be displayed in one slide, the chances for its success in the long term will be stifled.

The keys to success with governance and structure are simple. Leaders must ensure that a model exists. The model should be captured simply in a diagram of some sort. The organization's reporting structures should be outlined and detailed to include at minimum three layers: top leadership, divisional leadership and departments.

Most importantly, this information must be socialized and readily available to end users. There is only one constant in today's world: change. The more change occurs, the more risk increases. Thus, leaders must ensure that organizational changes in governance and structure are cascaded to stakeholders and displayed in a way that is relatable.

As Hosea (4:6, NIV) wrote, 'My people perish for a lack of knowledge.' The more leaders and staff know about how the organization is run and structured, the better.

3

The Power of the Knowledge Plan

Once the strategic planning process and organizational structure are defined and solidified, the next focal point is the knowledge plan. Organizational knowledge is synonymous with knowledge transfer and knowledge sharing. From a leadership perspective, organizational knowledge requires an assessment to ensure that the organization has the knowledge, skills and talent to meet customer expectations. The biggest pitfall some leaders make on this topic is focusing solely on succession planning. Yes, succession planning is an aspect of organizational knowledge. However, it is only one focus. There are many keys to successfully create, cultivate and implement a successful knowledge plan.

The purpose of this chapter is to outline the basic components of a knowledge plan. Again, plans depend upon the organization's size, scope, complexity and resourcing. However, the focus will be providing simple and tangible aspects of organizational knowledge that can be applied in any organization.

3.1 KNOWLEDGE DEFINITION

The first step in crafting a knowledge plan is to define what knowledge transfer means to the organization. Figure 3.1 outlines a simple example.

A simple definition of organizational knowledge is to transfer knowledge from one person to another, from one part of the organization to another and outside the organization. The key here is, for leaders, to land on the right definition for their enterprise. Next, leaders must identify potential knowledge transfer best practices of interest. There are many options, but the goal is to find the starting point, keep it simple and move forward.

DOI: 10.4324/9781003316251-3

FIGURE 3.1
Knowledge transfer defined.

Sample organizational knowledge focal points may include the following:

- *Coaching*—Some organizations have formal coaching programs. The most notable would be a formal executive coaching program. Here, top leaders and those aspiring top leaders are assigned a coach. These coaches are trained for this role. In some cases, the coaches may be employed by the organization. Often, the coaches are consultants that the organization hires from the outside specifically for training assignments. Either way, the key is to ensure that the coaches are unbiased, qualified and organized. These coaching engagements help leaders identify their strengths, obvious and hidden weakness and craft plans to improve their performance. The goal is improvement, gaining knowledge and leveraging this knowledge to make the organization and its processes better.
- *Work Shadowing*—Another viable option for knowledge plans is work shadowing or paired assignments. The key is to transfer knowledge across people groups. Common tactics include pairing new staff or leaders with those more experienced. The goal is to share knowledge, solidify the organization's culture, standardize operating norms and grow the level of understanding across the enterprise.
- *E-learning*—Some organizations invest in knowledge management systems. One aspect of these systems is the learning component. In healthcare, for example, these learning systems contain training modules for all staff that meet clinical and regulatory requirements. Staff and leaders may be trained on a variety of topics ranging from administering blood to understanding regulatory requirements tied to protected health information. The key is leveraging a system that

shares knowledge, tracks each candidate's progress and ensures that the knowledge is standardized. Often, leaders choose to require tests for the modules with minimum pass requirements to ensure that the knowledge was transferred and absorbed.

- *Quick Reference Guides*—Some organizations include short-form content as an aspect of their knowledge plans. Here, leaders and stakeholders document in simple forms or other formats how work is done. This is synonymous with job aids, instructions, quick guides and the like. The premise is simple. Document simply the right way to complete a task and make it readily available to others.

- *Knowledge Library*—The key is to capture knowledge, standardize it and make it readily available for end users when it is needed. Some organizations leverage a knowledge library or repository for this function. Simply put, leaders may choose to invest in a document management system that houses (in some instances) thousands of policies, procedures or work instruction, forms and other documents. Policies describe why we do something. The why is typically determined by regulatory requirements. Procedures are step-by-step instructions of how to do something. Forms are essential check sheets used for specific needs. Irrespective of the type of documentation utilized, the premise is to capture the organization's knowledge of how work is to be done correctly and catalog it, so end users can assess it when needed. The end goal is to create a culture of standard work.

- *Succession Planning*—The most common knowledge transfer focal point tends to be a succession plan. Here, leaders plan the talent pipeline for the future. The goal is to have a primary and backup person for each critical role—hence, the term 'critical role.' There are non-leadership roles that may not have direct reports that are critical to the organization's success. A good example would be an emergency management specialist. This person's role may be to help the organization plan for emergencies including natural disasters and man-made crises. Although it does not have any direct reports, it's vital to mission role. Thus, it should be included in the organization's succession plan. The key here is to identify all the critical roles, ensure that depth in these roles exists and share knowledge among the people groups so gaps don't arise.

3.2 TIMELINE AND TOLLGATE TEMPLATE

As noted in Figure 3.2, leaders must include a macro-timeline outlining specific tollgates in the knowledge plan. As noted, there are minimum five tollgates worth noting. First is the assessment and gap analysis. Leaders must determine where the organization's knowledge gaps exist based on the best practice focus areas. Common foci include high-turnover areas, documented knowledge, knowledge management systems, training programs, coaching engagements and the like.

Once gaps are identified, planning occurs. The knowledge plan should include various stakeholders ranging from operational leaders to strategists. It is important for the plans to be approved and socialized with all relevant stakeholders. Next, the plan is implemented and frequent reassessments occur. The goal is for leaders and responsible owners to determine what is working and what is not. Successes should be magnified, celebrated and modeled. In contrast, opportunities for improvement should be addressed quickly. For each tollgate, as noted in Figure 3.2, an associated timeline should be applied. The key is to create a roadmap, keep the organization on track and achieve the intended vision. A simple timeline is a great tool for knowledge progression.

3.3 KNOWLEDGE TRANSFER MIGRATION SHOWCASE

As noted in Figure 3.3, leaders should consider including a micro-focus or migration showcase. In this example, leaders outline the intended process or migration of its knowledge journey. For example, the leaders chose to focus on succession planning, turnover, cross training, shadowing,

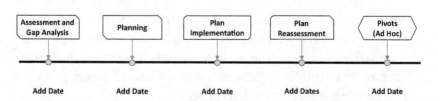

FIGURE 3.2
Timeline and tollgates' macro-view.

Person-to-Person

Succession Planning

Turnover*

Cross Training

Shadowing

Knowledge Management System

Depth in Roles

Quick Guides (Job Specific)

Dept-to-Dept

Succession Planning

Turnover*

Cross Training

Shadowing

Knowledge Management System

Depth in Roles

Quick Guides (Job Specific)

Enterprise Wide

Succession Planning

Turnover*

Cross Training

Shadowing

Knowledge Management System

Depth in Roles

Quick Guides (Job Specific)

External (International Scope)

Publications

Best Practice Programs

Webinars

Conceptual Models

Symposium Presentations

FIGURE 3.3
Knowledge transfer migration.

knowledge management system, depth in roles and quick guides. The migration is to start with person-to-person knowledge transfer on these topics. Then, migrate to department focus knowledge sharing. Next, share the knowledge and improve knowledge gaps enterprise-wide. Finally, the team plans to share knowledge externally via publications of lessons learned, presentations at industry venues and teach others what they learned on the journey. Figure 3.3 is a simple showcase of the starting point, focus areas and intended end.

3.4 KNOWLEDGE TRANSFER VISION SHOWCASE

In Figure 3.4, leaders should consider including a five-year vision. This vision focuses on organizational levels involved in the predetermined focus areas. As noted in the figure, all levels of the organization should be considered. For this example, the knowledge plan includes executives, divisional leaders, front-line leaders and front-line staff. The focus for year 1 is to ensure that the knowledge-plan focus areas are incorporated into the front-line leaders. Years 4 and 5 would begin to graft these attributes into the front-line staff. Years 2–5 would include the enterprise and divisional leaders.

The key is to ensure that a vision for implementing the knowledge focus areas exists, is captured in a simple showcase and involves all relevant stakeholders so the road ahead is clear and transparent.

3.5 KNOWLEDGE TRANSFER RISK ASSESSMENT

As with strategic planning, the knowledge plan should include a risk assessment per attribute. See Figure 3.5 for details and an example. As noted in the figure, there are six focus areas ranging from human resources to a surgery center for a hospital. Each focus area has a predetermined attribute as defined by the knowledge plan.

The attributes for this example are turnover, depth in roles, succession planning, e-learning and vacancy rates. It is imperative to note that leaders should measure each attribute over time (where applicable) and trend

Focus Area	Year 1	Year 2	Year 3	Year 4	Year 5
Enterprise-Level Leaders (Macro: Executives)		X	X	X	X
Divisional-Level Leaders (Meso: VP/AVP)		X	X	X	X
Front-Line-Level Leaders (Micro: Director/Manager)	X	X	X	X	X
Front-Line-Level Tenured Staff				X	X

FIGURE 3.4
Knowledge transfer vision.

Focus Area (Entity-Dept.)	Attribute	Risk (High/Medium/Low)	Owner
Human Resources	• Turnover	• High Risk	• Director
Facilities Mgmt	• Depth in Roles	• Medium Risk	• AVP
Nursing	• Turnover • Succession Planning • Orientation	• High Risk • Medium Risk • Low Risk	• Chief Nursing Officer
Supply Chain	• Turnover • E-learning	• Medium Risk • Low Risk	• AVP
Pharmacy	• Turnover • High Vacancy Rate	• Medium Risk • High Risk	• Director
Surgery Center	• Turnover	• High Risk	• AVP

• High Risk: Immediate Jeopardy to Life and Safety
• Medium Risk: Critical to Mission
• Low Risk: Important, but not Critical to Mission

FIGURE 3.5
Risk assessment.

performance to goal. Once identified, the attributes are risk assessed based on threat level to the organization.

There are three levels of risk identified. High-risk attributes are a direct threat to life and safety. Medium-risk attributes are critical to mission, but not a direct threat to life and safety. Low risks are important, but not critical to mission or a direct threat to life or safety. The key is for leaders to give priority to the high- and medium-risk attributes over the low-risk areas. Once risk assessed, each attribute is assigned to the responsible leader for resolution.

The takeaway for this template is simple. First, leaders should identify knowledge focus areas. Second, each area should focus on high-priority or high-risk attributes. Third, the organization should track and trend outcomes to a predetermined goal in the knowledge plan. For those areas meeting goal, full steam ahead. For those underperforming areas and attributes, a pivot is required and regular updates to the governing body are required.

3.6 KNOWLEDGE PLAN FIVE-YEAR FOCUS AREA TEMPLATE

One very important aspect of the knowledge plan is a five-year forward look at focus areas. As previously noted, knowledge focus areas are organization dependent and determined by respective leadership. In Figure 3.6, this example outlines focus areas for an enterprise ranging from turnover and succession planning to a knowledge library. The key is for leaders and the governing body to outline the priorities over the next five years. This will ensure that the organization has targets, stays on course and meets goals. Otherwise, the adage of 'driving blind' applies.

As the example displays, the leaders have decided to establish e-learning and the knowledge library in year 1. Starting in year 2, other focus areas come into play. Some focus areas such as turnover, succession planning and communication are a yearly focus each year. In contrast, paired work and coaching begin in year 2 and beyond.

Metric (Focus Area)	Year 1	Year 2	Year 3	Year 4	Year 5
Turnover	X	X	X	X	X
Succession Plan	X	X	X	X	X
Depth in Roles	X				
Cross Functional Training		X	X	X	X
E-Learning	X				
Paired Work			X	X	X
Communication Cascade	X	X	X	X	X
Onboarding	X				
Coaching		X	X	X	X
Knowledge Library	X				

FIGURE 3.6
Five-year focus areas.

The takeaway is for leaders to look ahead, plan for the future and have a plan. A multiyear focus and showcase are a good conversation starter and great addition to the enterprise knowledge plan.

3.7 REASSESSMENT TIMELINE TEMPLATE

As covered in Chapter 1, all planning should include reassessments. It is imperative for leaders to know if the plan is working or not. As noted in Figure 3.7, this is a monthly reassessment view. The key is for leaders to identify gaps of the plan, create a mitigation response and resolve the gaps quickly. Some attributes of the knowledge plan may require more frequent weekly or monthly reassessments. Again, the reassessment timeline will be organization dependent. However, the point is to look back frequently, magnify what worked and correct the gaps.

3.8 LESSONS LEARNED TEMPLATE

Figure 3.8 outlines a simple template for compiling lessons learned. Once the knowledge plan is implemented and reassessed, the team should

Month	Identified Gap(s)	Mitigation Plan	Owner	Gap Resolved? (Yes/No)
Jan				
Feb				
Mar				
Apr				
May				
June				
July				
Aug				
Sep				
Oct				
Nov				
Dec				

FIGURE 3.7
Reassessment timeline monthly.

complete a global after-action report for the enterprise. The first question to be answered is, what worked? Common considerations are as follows:

- Was the planning and implementation process effective?
- Did the knowledge plan work in correcting knowledge gaps?
- Were all the knowledge gaps identified?
- Were knowledge focus areas prioritized based on risk or threat to the organization appropriately?
- Were the high-risk focus areas given first priority or did leaders try to boil the ocean and fix everything at the same time?
- Was the knowledge plan communicated to all relevant stakeholders?
- Did leaders meet the knowledge-plan goals for each specific focus area?

The second question to answer is, what didn't work? The same questions as noted earlier apply here as well. The key is for leaders to ensure that there is a plan for what did not work. The plan should be correcting the non-conformity, sharing the lesson learned and preventing it from occurring again.

One often overlooked attribute of the look back process is ownership. It's imperative that each aspect of Figure 3.8 is assigned an owner for a couple of reasons: first, to ensure that wins are celebrated and due credit is given where deserved; second, to ensure that the opportunities are not lost in

What Worked?	What Didn't Work?	Plan for What Didn't Work	Owner

FIGURE 3.8
Lessons learned.

other organizational priorities. At the end of the knowledge-plan process, the goal is for everyone to be successful, transfer knowledge and ensure that the organization is primed for long-term relevancy.

The keys to success for knowledge-plan implementation are as follows:

1. Everyone knows the plan, process and their role.
2. Everyone contributes to success.
3. Everyone contributes to excellence.
4. Everyone has a safe place to succeed or fail with the expectation to try again if failure results.
5. Wins are celebrated by top leadership and the governing body.
6. Communication of the plan, process and progress is regular and reaches all stakeholders.
7. Knowledge gaps are corrected when identified.

4

The Knowledge of Leadership Maturity

4.1 MODELING LEADERSHIP MATURITY: IS LEADERSHIP IMMATURE, GROWING, OR FULLY BAKED?

Maturity can be defined as a state of being 'fully developed' (1). This concept is also synonymous with being ripe, growth, advancement and perfected. The key is that maturity takes time, which requires development. From a leadership perspective, leadership is a risky business.

Leadership is often related to holding a position, possessing a title, wielding authority over others and the like. However, is a leader accurately defined by these attributes? The short answer is not always. True leaders are those that have influence with others. Moreover, a simple test of a leader is to gauge if they have followers. At the end of the day, leadership is simply getting others to do what you want without force.

So, why do so many organizations plus current and aspiring leaders struggle with this concept? Why do some leaders get promoted early and last while others do not? Why do some leaders never mature in the leadership arena? Why are some leaders promoted before they are fully developed and get crushed by the weight of the leadership stage? Why do some leaders mature rapidly and stand the test of time?

The simplest answer lies in measurement. For leaders and organizations to know who to promote and when, a maturity model is needed. The worst thing for a leader is to be promoted before they are ready. Equally tragic is for organizations not to identify talent that are mature and ripe for the next level? In this scenario, organizations will lose top talent to the next highest

DOI: 10.4324/9781003316251-4

bidder. The key is to measure leadership maturity, cultivate talent at the right stage and promote mature leaders when they are ready for the next level.

4.1.1 Leadership Maturity Model

As noted in Figure 4.1, there are eight levels of leadership maturity.

The first level begins with base education and skills. Here, leaders complete training and degrees for their respective career field. Leaders learn the basics which essentially unlocks the door to entry-level positions via meeting minimum job requirements. The goal is to gain access to the leadership realm so maturity can continue.

The second level of leadership maturity, as noted in Figure 4.1, relates to initial wins. Once leaders have mastered the basics of working with others, leading basic initiatives and learning organizational culture, they begin to amass a list of initial wins. These wins don't have to be earth shaking

1. • **Basic Education + Skills**
2. • **Initial Wins**
3. • **Integrated Skill Set**
4. • **Cross Functional Wins**
5. • **Sustained Success**
6. • **Team Building**
7. • **Knowledge Transfer**
8. • **Persona**

FIGURE 4.1
Leadership maturity model.

or industry-leading inventions. Simply put, leaders just need to show that they can set and meet goals for high-priority initiatives.

Once leaders prove that they can win in tough environments, they continue to learn and grow with the integrated skill set. Here, leaders move outside of their comfort zone or technical prowess. A good example would be a nurse in healthcare. The nurse spent several years attaining a nursing degree and working in the clinical arena to master clinical skills.

A few years later, the nurse earns a master's degree in business and is promoted to a department director position. This exposure provides operational experience and competencies by leading others, solving problems, successfully managing budgets and the like. Next, the leader earns a Lean or Six Sigma credential. With time, the leader begins to solve process problems in their department such as delays, errors and reworks. The wins amass over time and realize hard dollar savings.

In short, the integrated skill set encompasses technical and operational leadership and performance improvement skill sets with significant outcomes. The key here is significant outcomes. As has been said often, 'Activity without outcomes is a waste of time.' Thus, leaders that have an integrated skill set with measurable success are ripe for the next opportunity.

The fourth level of leadership maturity relates to cross-functional wins. Here, leaders have the skill and experience to solve problems outside their comfort zone (i.e., area of training). This is a direct indicator of leadership growth. Leaders branch out of their area of training to address issues and create solutions in unfamiliar territory.

Let's revisit the nurse example previously noted. Once the nurse masters the integrated skill set, the nurse receives a stretch assignment to address delays in billing. The nurse has never worked in the financial arena. However, the nurse successfully leads an interdisciplinary team to reduce thousands of billing errors which in turn realizes millions of dollars in hard savings.

The fifth level of the leadership maturity focuses on sustained success. Here, a very important question is answered. Is success really success? The key is that success, goal attainment, breakthrough wins and the like must be sustained for long term. Without sustainability, wins are questionable at best and arguable as not true success.

The sixth level of the model relates to team building. Once leaders have proven that they have the 'chops' to win in various arenas and sustain those improvements for a long term, the leadership test shifts. This shift focuses on the ability to build teams. In essence, a leader's maturity is directly correlated with the ability to grow the pie, build cohesive teams, gain synergies where the team leverages its strengths that cover its weaknesses and the like. The key for leadership maturity is to ensure that the team accomplishes more together than as individuals. Moreover, mature leaders possess the ability to ensure that teams are positioned for long-term success by sharing knowledge to develop the team which in turn grows the pie of success for all stakeholders.

The seventh level of leadership maturity centers around knowledge transfer. Here, leaders enter the thought leadership arena. Years ago, an aspiring change agent and thought leader said, 'I get paid to think.' Unfortunately, this was a short-cited view.

Thought leadership does entail thinking. However, true thought leaders possess the ability to transition thought into knowledge that is passed on to others inside and outside the organization. The test at this stage is if the leader can publish their best practice outcomes, impact the industry body of knowledge, become recognized as an industry leader and impact external industries. The degree to which knowledge transfer grows will directly impact the leader's maturity.

The final level of the leadership maturity model is persona. In simplest of terms, how does the leader handle success? Is success a motivator to help others or does the leader become more self-absorbed and self-centered? Arguably, this is the biggest test of leadership that must be passed. Leadership maturity will be readily recognizable by a simple phrase: 'I' or 'me' versus 'We' or 'Us.' If leaders focus on 'we' or 'us' by growing the pie for others, then they mature. In contrast, if leaders focus on 'I' or 'me,' then they rot on the vine and fail to mature.

4.1.2 Leadership Maturity Evolution Action Plan

As organizations and leaders assess their leadership maturity, it's imperative to translate the maturity level to an action plan. See Figure 4.2 for details.

As noted, leaders focusing on basic skills and initial wins are categorized as basic or immature. Here, the leaders should be cultivated, be mentored, paired with senior leader sponsors and coached. Unfortunately, promotion at this level would be a high-risk proposition and produce bitter fruit that is not fully ripened.

Leaders that have achieved the integrated skill set, cross-functional wins and sustained these successes can be categorized as growing. Here, the

Maturity Anchor	Leader Maturity Level	Action Plan
Base Education + Skills Initial Wins	Basic or Immature	• Cultivate; Mentor; Pair with Sponsor; Coach
Integrated Skill Set Cross Functional Wins Sustained Success	Growing	• Test; Grow; Stretch Assignments; Promote; Coach
Team Building Knowledge Transfer Persona	Mature	• Model; Champion; Team Build; Increase Influence; Promote; Coach

FIGURE 4.2
Leadership maturity evolution action plan.

prescription or action plan matures and is expanded. These leaders should be constantly tested to see exactly how much responsibility or pressure they can handle. These tests may take the form of cyclical stretch assignments outside the comfort zone. The end goal is to accelerate maturity, grow the leader and ready them for the next-level promotion. The quicker they mature in this phase, the sooner they should be promoted. It's also important to continue coaching during this phase so the leaders stay on track and progress as expected.

Finally, when leaders begin to master team building, knowledge transfer and persona, the action plan should accelerate growth and promotion. Here, these leaders should evolve quickly into organizational champions and leadership models for others to follow. The adage of 'trend setter' applies here. The action plan includes a heavy focus on team building. These leaders must evolve into master builders of organizational talent. The key is to grow teams, transfer knowledge, cultivate influence across the enterprise and coach others for success. It's a reasonable expectation that these leaders would assume senior-level leadership roles.

4.1.3 Lessons Learned

Looking back at the leadership maturity model, let's answer some of the original considerations:

- ***Why do so many organizations plus current and aspiring leaders struggle with this concept?*** The simple answer is many fail to properly assess, measure and understand the maturity of their talent pipelines.

This was witnessed years ago when an up-and-coming leader was promoted several levels successively within a short time frame to a senior leadership role. The leader was good with organizational politics and won the favor of many senior leaders. However, it was only at level 2 on the maturity model (see Figure 4.1). The leader was simply not prepared for the weight of the stage and crumbled. The leader struggled to establish cross-functional wins and to sustain success for a long term. Moreover, transferring knowledge and the persona were off the mark. Thus, the leader's failure and fall were faster than their rise. As noted, one of the worst things an organization can do is promoting a leader before they are ripe, developed and mature.

- **Why do some leaders get promoted early and last while others do not?** Simply put, some leaders mature faster than others. As noted in Figure 4.1, some leaders have the ability to learn, apply what is learned and grow the pie for others at a faster rate. Also, these fast trackers realize early on that leadership is about sharing knowledge, helping others be their best and growing the pie instead of falling prey to the 'I' or 'me' persona.
- **Why do some leaders never mature in the leadership arena?** The simplest answer is that some leaders build their brand on politics instead of measurable outcomes. As noted in Figure 4.1, there is no level for political prowess. Yes, managing relationships is a part of leadership regardless of industry. However, leaders that build their brand out of the ability to win favor with others will ultimately fail. Years ago, a forward-thinking thought leader branded these leaders as, 'All pop, no fizz.' When times get tough, organizations will be forced to align with leaders that can lead from the front, solve problems in various arenas, build teams, sustain wins, transfer knowledge and focus on the big picture. The old adages of 'talk is cheap' and 'actions speak louder than words' most definitely apply here.

4.1.4 Summary

Leadership is a journey and risky proposition. It's not for the faint of heart. Leadership maturity requires time. Often, many leaders or those aspiring lack the patience to complete the maturity journey. Instead, they jump from vine to vine while they are ill prepared and only last for a short time.

Effective leaders are those that understand, measure and grow their maturity over time. Moreover, effective organizations are those that measure, grow and mature their talent pipeline. The key is measurement. Ignorance is never bliss. We don't know what is not measured.

Leadership maturity is a balancing act. On one hand, if a leader is promoted too soon, they will be unripe or underprepared and ultimately fail. Similarly, if the organization doesn't promote ripe leaders at the right time, they will be harvested by the competition. Understanding leadership maturity and leveraging a maturity model are key ingredients to long-term success, market viability and reaping the desired leadership harvest.

REFERENCE

1. Dictionary.com, 2021

5

The Power of Measuring Organizational Knowledge

DOI: 10.4324/9781003316251-5

5.1 IS A NORMAL DISTRIBUTION A RISKY PROPOSITION WITH ORGANIZATIONAL KNOWLEDGE?

5.1.1 Knowledge Defined

Knowledge can be defined as 'Understanding and skill gained by experience' (1). The reality is that knowledge is derivative of time and people. Knowledge or wisdom is gained over time through experiences, training, development, tests and trials. The adage of 'nothing comes easy' definitely applies here.

Unfortunately, organizational knowledge is one of the snazzy tag lines often used by thought leaders that is greatly misunderstood and underestimated. From a holistic perspective, organizational knowledge is synonymous with knowledge sharing, knowledge transfer and the like. Far too often, leaders perceive this topic to only apply to succession planning. In reality, organizational knowledge is much more far-reaching and impactful.

For the sake of this conversation, let's use the tag line knowledge transfer as the focus area. Organizational knowledge transfer is simply transferring knowledge from one person to another, from one business unit to another, across the enterprise (cross functionally) and outside the organization. There are many techniques to transfer knowledge, but the key is measurement.

Some organizations focus their talent development (i.e., knowledge transfer) efforts on various techniques. One way to share knowledge is through cross training. Here, leaders and staff are allowed to learn other roles and responsibilities outside of their normal role. With time, this exposure to other people, processes and aspects of the business grow knowledge.

Organizations may also develop their knowledge by investing in a knowledge management system. This system typically houses the organization's written knowledge in the form of policies, procedures and the like. The end goal is for leaders and staff to have a well of knowledge in which they can quickly retrieve organizational processes which outline how work should be done in the specific area and role. The measure of success is for work to be completed the right way each and every time. The key is to ensure that the knowledge is standardized, readily accessible and organized.

A third knowledge transfer technique often used is coaching. Here, leaders, for example, are coached on best practices such as emotional intelligence, relationship management and executive presence. The goal is for the coach and leader to identify strengths and weaknesses and create a road map to help the leader mature and grow in knowledge. Common techniques to grow the leader's knowledge may be recommendations for training, education, role playing, pairing with a sponsor or senior leader and personality assessments, just to name a few. Simply put, organizations may use this technique to grow their leaders and subsequently the knowledge of the organization.

As previously noted, a very common knowledge-sharing technique is succession planning. Here, organizations include knowledge into their strategic plans. The first step is assessing the current state. Common considerations may include the following. Where is the core knowledge located? Do we have knowledge gaps? Are we able to hire the right knowledge and retain it? Is knowledge being transferred from one generation to the other? Is knowledge being documented and stored in a knowledge management system? Is culture aligned with the ideal knowledge state correlated with expected values, norms and cultural expectations?

It is common and a good idea to objectively measure each consideration with data. Common data sets may include, but not be limited to: turnover rates, vacancy rates, seniority levels and performance evaluation outcomes just to name a few. In particular, some organizations may consider the distribution of performance outcomes across the enterprise to identify where the top performers reside and ensure that their knowledge is being transferred to others.

Once the current state is assessed, organizations create and implement plans to ensure that knowledge is present, cultivated and equally distributed across the enterprise. Moreover, cultural alignment must occur to ensure that the knowledge gaps are filled and values become a reality instead of just a talking point. The end goal is to achieve higher levels of operational performance to ensure organizational viability in the long term via hiring, developing and promoting the right talent (i.e., knowledge).

A common tactic for knowledge-plan execution is the performance-based incentive program. Here, the organization evaluates all leaders and staff at minimum annually on performance to values, goals and the like. Higher performance in theory denotes a higher ranking, vice versa. Those top performers and champions of ideal cultural expectations are rewarded with training, stretch assignments, promotions, pay incentives and other opportunities to solidify organizational knowledge transfer.

In some cases, some leaders strive for and use a normal distribution in talent development. As noted in Figure 5.1, a normal distribution is simply a bell-shaped curve statistically. Here, 68% of the values fall within one standard deviation of the mean. Also, 99.5% fall within two standard

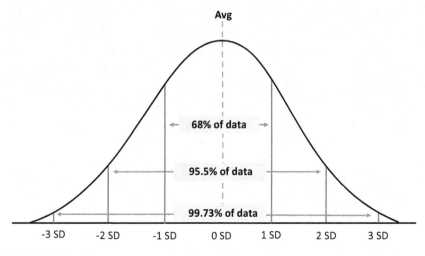

FIGURE 5.1
Normal distribution curve.

deviations from the mean and 99.73% fall within three standard deviations from the mean. In simplest of terms, leaders may strive to ensure that 70% or more of the leaders and staff are higher performers with lower performers making up the difference.

This sounds good in theory. However, is a normal distribution as it relates to organizational knowledge a risky proposition? Let's take a closer look at a case study to learn more.

5.1.2 Case Study

A consulting team was engaged to assist a top leader in the service industry to develop an organizational knowledge plan. The organization had a large geographic footprint and many large business units. The goal was to leverage the performance-based incentive program to ensure that the right talent was hired, cultivated and promoted. The program was focused on an annual assessment of all leaders and staff.

The performance-based evaluations rated each stakeholder on their adherence to organizational values and goal attainment. The goals were tied to larger organizational goals and the values were solidified and approved by the governing body. The top leader presumed by incorporating values such as teamwork, integrity and excellence into the performance evaluation system that this tool would reshape the organization's culture with better alignment to the industry landscape or future direction.

An initial conversation with the consulting team included goals of the engagement, direction and the top leader's vision for the performance-based incentive program. The leader mandated that 70% of the leaders and staff had to be rated as value adds, 20% had to be rated as higher performers and 10% had to be rated as low performers. The vision was for the organization as a whole to meet this distribution of knowledge.

The focal point was value. Think of the value equation (quality plus service divided cost). Higher performers were those leaders, for example, that meet and exceeded goals tied to customer satisfaction, quality of services and costs. The best of this subgroup would have to exceed goals plus complete successful stretch assignments outside their work area. This subgroup would be aligned for promotions and other knowledge-sharing opportunities.

Value add leaders were those that met goals tied to the value equation. Here, the leaders made up the majority of the organization and were the bearers of the organization's culture. Think of 'backbone' leaders that keep the business running each day. This subgroup was aligned to be developed and cultivated for higher levels of responsibility.

The lower performers were those that struggled with performance outcomes. In short, they failed to consistently meet goals tied to value and/or did not meet value expectations. The goal with this subgroup was to save those that could be improved with coaching and management plans. Those that were not viable candidates for transformation were transitioned out of the enterprise. It was also implied and expected that all leaders would meet values each year.

As the team's work progressed, the mandate was cascaded to all leaders. Annual performance evaluations were conducted annually following the normal distribution theory. All business units ensured that their evaluations mirrored the 70/20/10 distribution for their direct report populations. Unfortunately, not all performance mirrored the distribution, and leaders found themselves forcing the distribution on the staff and leader populations.

As time passed, the organization's outcomes declined significantly. The team conducted an after-action assessment for further clarity as to why the organization's path did not mirror the plan. As noted in Figure 5.2, the organization's goal attainment tied to service, cost and quality sharply declined over a few years. The normal distribution requirement for performance evaluations was implemented in year 1, as shown in Figure 5.2.

As noted in the figure, each year the organization's value outcomes declined. By tenth year, there was a 40% reduction in annual operational goal attainment as compared to year 1 when the normal distribution requirement was implemented. The annual financial impact was in the tens of millions of dollars (unfavorable). Over the period, the organization lost hundreds of millions of dollars due to the operational decline.

Similarly, the goal was for 70% of the leaders to meet value goals. In reality, only 45% of the leaders met their annual goals. However, 70% of the population was rated as value adds. The gap for this subgroup was 25%. This meant that 25% of the leaders were given a higher rating than they deserved in this subgroup.

The low performers had the biggest performance gap. The goal was, for the enterprise, to only have 10% of its population that needed to improve

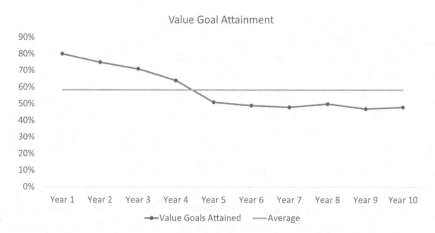

FIGURE 5.2

The team placed the goal attainment data in a control chart as noted in Figure 5.3. It was discovered that the goal data were out of control for the period. Moreover, there was a downward shift in goals attained in years 5–10 as noted in Figure 5.3. Simply put, the environment was riddled with special cause variation indicating that system issues were present. This was a signal that the operational downturn was real and course correction was needed immediately. The adage of 'crisis negotiation' applies here.

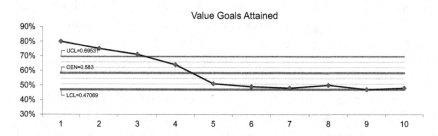

FIGURE 5.3

The team then began the reassessment of the performance evaluation system to find root causes, drivers and correlations between the mandate and operational declines. As noted in Figure 5.4, notable gaps were present.

performance. In reality, 50% of the population was not able to meet its value goals. Thus, a 40% gap in performance existed.

Globally speaking, the distribution goal combining higher performers and value adds was for 90% of the leaders to meet and exceed goals. In reality, only 50% of the leaders actually met or exceeded the performance outcome requirements. Thus, a 50% buffer in the system existed.

Category	Distribution Goal	Actual Performance	Distribution Gap
High Performers	20%	5%	−15%
Value Adds	70%	45%	−25%
Low Performers	10%	50%	40%

FIGURE 5.4

The goal was for 20% of the leaders to be rated as higher performers. However, in reality, only 5% of the leadership population was able to meet and exceed goals tied to value. This left a 15% gap in higher performers' outcomes. This meant that 15% of the population was given a top performer rating when they failed to meet the requirements.

In layman's terms, leaders were being overrated for their outcomes. Lower performers were being promoted unjustifiably. As a result, the organization's performance declined as actual lower performers were promoted. The end result was an inverse reward system which created and reshaped the operational landscape unfavorably.

5.1.3 Lessons Learned

There are several lessons learned from the case study. First, organizational leaders did not realize that the elephant in the room was organizational knowledge. Knowledge transfer is much more than just creating a talent pipeline or mechanism to identify top talent. The process must include identifying knowledge gaps, then applying solutions to grow knowledge. The key is to align culture properly. Leaders must ensure that theory will create the ideal reality.

Second, measurement is the key to succeed in the knowledge arena. Leaders simply don't know what they don't measure. Ignorance is never bliss. Without proper situational awareness, perception may become an unexpected reality. In the case study, the top leader presumed that a normal distribution was ideal. However, in reality, the normal distribution did not exist and leaders forced the distribution on a population with dire consequences.

Third, leaders must go back to the basics. Simple data display can decipher truth from fiction at a glance if leveraged properly. The key is for leaders to display data over time to goal. There are three questions to answer when viewing data. Are we meeting goal? Are we improving to achieve goal? Are the data in or out of control?

The simplest tools for this are a run chart and a control chart. However, leaders must know what the display is telling them. As noted in the case study, the data declined immediately and were out of control. These signals would have saved the organization hundreds of millions of dollars if realized and understood early on. Again, ignorance is never bliss.

Finally, leaders must use statistical theory carefully. In this case, forcing a normal distribution was catastrophic. Theory is only an assumption until proven to be a viable reality. Leaders must proceed with caution in designing concepts and models. Otherwise, people will be harmfully impacted, organizations will fail and humanity will suffer.

5.1.4 Summary

Organizational knowledge is one of the most important aspects of leadership. As Hosea (4:1, NIV) wrote, 'My people are destroyed for a lack of knowledge.' Unfortunately, many leaders succumb to the pitfall of not realizing the elephant in the room until it's too late. The takeaway is that organizational knowledge is a risky proposition. Also, presuming that a normal distribution is ideal for all knowledge landscapes may be presumptive. The key is for leaders to understand their situation, leverage data, display signals and heed the warnings before it's too late. Not knowing is costly, harmful and impactful to humanity in immeasurable ways.

REFERENCE

1. Merriam-Webster, 2021

6

The Power of Knowledge Gaps

6.1 KNOWLEDGE GAPS: BRIDGING THE DIVIDE WITH INSIGHT, FORETHOUGHT, AND MEASUREMENT

6.1.1 Organizational Knowledge

Organizational knowledge can be defined as 'The different knowledge and skills that the employees of a large company or organization have, and how these can be used and shared to make the organization more effective' (1). Knowledge is arguably one the most important determinants of organizational success. In some thought leadership circles, this topic is often referred to as knowledge transfer or knowledge sharing. However, is organizational knowledge only tied to transferring or sharing knowledge? The short answer is not always.

For organizations and their leaders to fully understand the concept of knowledge, a process is needed. See Figure 6.1 for details.

In short, knowledge transfer begins with an assessment. Here, leaders assess the current state of knowledge that exists in the enterprise. The assessment should include both the location and presence of knowledge banks and knowledge gaps. Knowledge banks are ideal hot spots where high levels of organizational knowledge exist. In contrast, knowledge gaps are voids or gray areas in the enterprise where organizational knowledge is lacking. The key is to assess all areas in the enterprise from front lines to C-Suite. Unfortunately, top leaders often overlook many front-line critical positions and focus mainly on the upper echelon. Thus, knowledge gaps and banks go undiscovered or are often underrepresented.

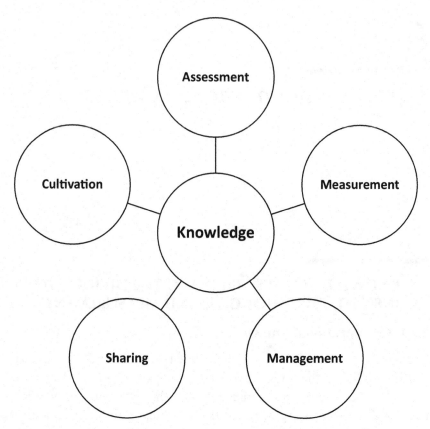

FIGURE 6.1
Organizational knowledge components.

Part of the assessment must include some level of measurement. Leaders don't know what they don't measure. Thus, the organization should measure attributes such as tenure or seniority levels, processes of how work is done in the enterprise, training attributes, turnover rates, education levels and the like. The goal is to measure the organization's knowledge levels and gain a better understanding of where gaps exist.

Third, thought leaders must manage organizational knowledge. Here, high-performing organizations capture the organization's knowledge in a knowledge management system. One aspect of the system will include documented processes of how work is done in various work areas. This documented knowledge may take the form of policies, procedures or work instructions and forms to start. The goal is to capture as many of the organization's processes as possible, standardize the processes in templates, organize them electronically and leverage a knowledge system for storage and retrieval by end users. The test of success here is the organization's ability to document its processes and make them readily available for all end users as needed.

Next, thought leaders must share knowledge. There is one pitfall to avoid. Thought leaders must ensure that the scope of knowledge sharing exceeds the four walls of the enterprise. In its simplest form, knowledge transfer encompasses how well the organization transfers knowledge from one person to another, from one business unit to another and across the enterprise. This is commonly referred to as internal knowledge transfer. Common techniques may include training courses, stretch assignments, paired work where experienced and inexperienced leaders collaborate, leveraging various communication channels, mentoring and the like. The key is for internal stakeholders at all levels to learn, grow their knowledge bases and share what they have learned to others.

Similarly, leaders should consider external knowledge transfer. This concept occurs when leaders and/or the organization as a whole share knowledge outside the organization. Common techniques may include presentations at industry seminars, publishing best practice outcomes, developing and publishing new concepts or models and teaching classes at formal education venues just to name a few. The goal here is to impact the body of knowledge and help others improve from lessons learned inside the enterprise.

Once leaders understand where knowledge gaps exist, capture as much of the organization's knowledge as possible in written form and share lessons learned, they must then cultivate or grow the knowledge base. One of the most common techniques is succession planning or depth in roles. Here, the organization's top leaders strategize, plan and cultivate a talent pipeline. The intent is to ensure that the organization currently has the talent needed to meet customer expectations and will continue to do so in the future. Since people are the bearers of organizational knowledge, the selection process of top leadership is a crucial attribute for long-term success and market viability. As Hosea (4:1, NIV) wrote, 'My people die for a lack of knowledge.' Thus, succession planning is fundamental knowledge cultivation technique.

6.1.2 Knowledge Gap Risk Factors

Along with knowledge gaps, thought leaders must consider knowledge risk factors. See Figure 6.2 for details.

From a micro-level, leaders must assess each critical role regardless of its position, height or depth on the organizational chart. First, leaders must consider the roles market demands. Those roles in high demand are of higher risk to the organization. As demand increases for skill sets, so does (typically) compensation. Thus, high-demand roles are more attractive and pose higher flight risks for top performers.

The second knowledge risk relates to market supply for specific roles. Here, leaders must understand the current market landscape. Is the supply of leaders for the specific role in consideration high or low? Here, low supply for critical or highly valued roles is high risk. When talent is plentiful, risk is low. Again, thought leaders should master the art and science of

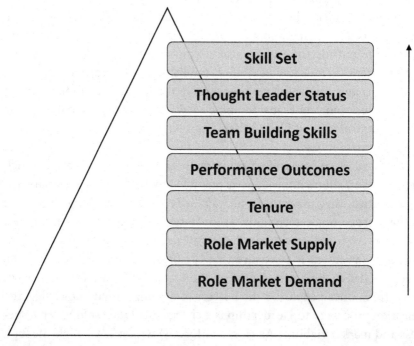

FIGURE 6.2
Knowledge-gap risk factors.

microeconomics to leverage talent pipeline demand and supply. Otherwise, ignorance will be bliss until the organization is unexpectantly disrupted.

The third knowledge-gap risk relates to tenure. Tenure can be an elusive concept. However, in simplest terms, leaders must understand how many years the organization can expect current leaders are expected to stay with the organization. Those with longer tenure are closer to retirement, thus a higher flight risk. Moreover, those higher performers with reasonable tenure are also at higher risk as they are attractive to competitors.

The next knowledge risk factor relates to performance outcomes. Is the leader(s) in question a high performer? Does he/she meet and exceed goals tied to service, cost and quality as compared to peers? Does the leader excel in team-building capabilities? Can the leader predictably and consistently build teams that outperform their colleagues? If so, then the leader(s) in question is at high risk. Simply put, those that can meet more goals and produce better outcomes consistently than peers will be more attractive to competitors and have more career choice.

The final and often overlooked knowledge risk factors are thought leader status and integrated skill sets. This concept is simpler than it sounds. In today's market, those leaders who possess an integrated skill set are typically better performers, more recognized and considered more widely to be thought leaders. The integrated skill set consists of technical and operational leadership and performance improvement skills with associated significant outcomes.

Moreover, these influencers tend to be master change agents with a successful track record of cross-functional wins as well. A good test of a true thought leader is their ability to solve problems, create innovative solutions, publish outcomes and share knowledge across various industries. The key here is that established thought leaders are at higher risk than their counterparts. As their knowledge grows, so does their value and scarcity. Thus, the demand and compensation for those skills increases. Simply put, they quickly become highly valued targets for competition to draft them away from the organization.

6.1.3 Knowledge Gap Side Effects

Often, leaders and their organizations underestimate the impact of knowledge gaps. When knowledge is lacking, the work environment can easily become dysfunctional and chaotic. For example, if the organization has high top leadership turnover, each transition can reduce morale, increase turnover at various levels and negatively impact value. In simplest terms, value relates to service, cost and quality of services.

Also, an unfortunate and widely overlooked side effect of knowledge gaps is inadvertent gap filling. This occurs when opportunists take advantage of a knowledge gap or gray area. For example, if an organization experiences a restructure and critical leadership roles are vacant for a prolonged period of time, lower performers may be leveraged to fill the gap. Moreover, in precarious situations, some leaders that are not equipped for the roles may finagle a situation to take advantage of a knowledge gray area. In the short run, the leader in question may benefit due to a promotion. However, in the long run, the organization will be impacted negatively due to underperformance, decreased morale, turnover of other top performers, disengagement of backbone leaders and other value-related issues that may arise due to leadership lacking knowledge.

Let's take a closer look at an example where knowledge was lacking and leaders simply didn't know what they didn't know.

6.1.4 Case Study

A large service organization was high performing historically. Over a decade or so, the organization experienced several disruptions that significantly shifted its trajectory in the wrong direction. One disruptor related directly to organizational knowledge. The enterprise, as a whole, historically had low turnover and high levels of tenure at all levels.

As time passed, the enterprise at all levels experienced higher than normal turnover that increased over time. The organization went from annual turnover rates less than 15% to over 20% for all business units. The annual cost impact alone was over $20 million due to knowledge loss. For each critical role that left the enterprise, the cost effect per role was over 100% of the salary for that role. This includes cost of poor quality due to knowledge loss and vacancies, hiring, training, orientation costs and the like.

This trend also included top leadership. The upper echelon experienced over 30% turnover rates during this period as well. The industry average for the time was less than 20%. With each top leader turnover, the organization's morale, engagement and stability took a nosedive. Annual engagement and employee satisfaction surveys hit all-time lows for consecutive years running.

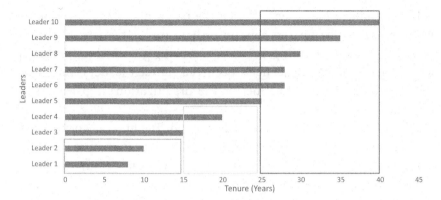

FIGURE 6.3
Top leader tenure.

A thought-leader change agent was engaged to assess the situation and collaborate with top leadership to help resolve the trend. To start, the thought leader used a simple knowledge-gap assessment tool. See Figure 6.3 for details.

The tool listed the top leaders in the enterprise by tenure in the role or their career tenure (whichever was longer).

The goal was to determine which leaders were at highest risk to leave their roles. As noted in Figure 6.3, there were three zones. The red zone represented those top leaders that were within three to five years of retirement. This red zone was the most critical designation and the highest risk category. Sixty percent of the top leaders were at high risk.

The yellow zone represented medium risk. Those top leaders with 15 to 25 years of tenure fell into this category. The yellow zone leaders were at medium flight risks due to tenure. However, they were also at moderate risk to leave based on their experience levels. These leaders were highly prized as they had good experience and were beginning to produce highly prized outcomes. Twenty percent of the organization's top leaders resided in this category.

The green zone in the figure represented low-risk leaders. Here, the leaders had less than 15 years of tenure. Thus, they were still learning, growing and produced the least risk for leaving their posts. Twenty percent of the enterprise leaders were categorized as the green-zone low-risk leaders.

The thought leader then assessed the talent pipeline. This pipeline was represented by up and coming early to mid-careerists. In theory, these leaders were learning, growing and being groomed to fill the top leadership roles when vacancies occurred. Fifteen leaders were identified as being in the pipeline for the organization's top leadership pipeline.

There were three categories of leaders found. The first category of pipeline leaders was 'knowledge gap.' These leaders were immature in tenure, knowledge, skill and outcomes. They simply were not ready to be promoted and they assume a top leadership role.

The next category was classified as 'still growing.' Here, the leaders had moderate tenure, skill and outcomes. However, they too were not fully ripe as thought leaders or prepared to handle a top leadership assignment. The third category was classified as 'Viable Candidate.' These leaders were in the top leadership talent pipeline and ready for the next-level role based on knowledge, skill and outcomes.

The thought leader then completed a cross comparison of the knowledge gaps for the top leaders as noted in Figure 6.3 to the identified talent pipeline. See Figure 6.4 for details.

As noted, only 20% of the top leaders were stable or expected to remain in their roles for more than three to five years. Eighty percent of the top leaders were at moderate to high risk.

Similarly, 67% of the talent pipeline leaders were not ready (i.e., knowledge gaps) for the next-level role. Only 13% of these cohorts were ready to fill a top leadership role if needed. As noted in Figure 6.4, the organization's knowledge gap for top leadership was 60%. In layman's terms, it simply means that there was no succession plan for 60% of the organization's top leaders. If those leaders vacated their role for any reason, a replacement was not readily available to fill the knowledge gap. Thus, unfavorable outcomes tied to value, cost, quality, service and organizational talent were to be expected.

The takeaway from the case study is that knowledge matters. The organization did not assess, measure or understand its risk as it related to organizational knowledge. Most of the top leaders were at high risk and the organization failed to cultivate a talent pipeline to mitigate those risks. The expected end was simple. The thought leader projected that the turnover, value underperformance and operational issues would continue at historic rates. Unfortunately, this is exactly what happened.

	Count	%
Stable Top Leaders	2	20%
High-Risk Top Leaders	8	80%
Pipeline Leaders Ready	2	13%
Pipeline Leaders Growing	3	20%
Pipeline Leaders Not Ready	10	67%
Knowledge Gap (Leaders)	6	60%

*Current Top Leaders (n=10)
**Pipeline Leaders (n=15)

FIGURE 6.4
Knowledge gap.

6.1.5 Mitigation Strategies

When faced with knowledge gaps, there are a few countermeasures organizations should consider to lower the risk. First, thought leaders must ensure that the enterprise has a solid, cyclical and well-thought-out strategic planning process. This process should occur at minimum annually. Part of the process should include a knowledge-gap analysis. Once gaps are identified, plans should be implemented to fill the knowledge gaps. Outcomes to goal should be measured, reported to the governing body and benchmarked against best practices.

Second, thought leaders must create and expand their organization's knowledge plan. This plan may include succession plans for all levels, a knowledge management system, cross training, organizational learning and many other attributes too numerous to mention. The end goal is to ensure that the organization understands where its knowledge is, where it is lacking and has a plan to fill the knowledge gaps.

Third, leaders must ensure that a talent pipeline exists and is adequate to meet the organization's short-term and long-term needs. Here, the organization must measure the current state, project future talent needs based on past trends and make evidence-based decisions to ensure that knowledge is available across the enterprise. It takes years to develop leaders. Talent development does not occur over night. Therefore, leaders must understand the organization's talent risks, plan ahead and cultivate knowledge, so gaps are avoided.

6.1.6 Summary

Organizational knowledge is fast becoming one of the hottest thought leadership topics. Unfortunately, many leaders silo this topic into a single lens focused mainly on succession planning. Knowledge transfer, as noted in Figure 6.4, is multifactor including process, structure, technology and most importantly people. People are the bearers of organizational knowledge and culture. Thus, knowledge transfer should center on the people the organization currently needs, will need in the future and their gaps or banks of knowledge.

The takeaway is that organizational viability and longevity are predicted on the level of knowledge it possesses, creates and cultivates over time. Effective leaders are those that know their knowledge gaps, leverage knowledge banks, develop viable talent pipelines and never get left not knowing what is over the horizon. The key to effectively managing talent is bridging the knowledge divide with insight, forethought and measurement.

REFERENCE

1. Cambridge Dictionary, 2021. https://dictionary.cambridge.org/us/dictionary/english/organizational-knowledge

7

The Power of Knowledge in Leadership Decisions

7.1 THE LEADERSHIP FORKS IN THE ROAD: SMOOTH SAILING OR DEAD END AHEAD?

7.1.1 Leadership Defined

Leadership can be defined as 'The power or ability to lead other people' (1). This concept denotes that some level of action is required to be a leader. Leadership is synonymous with being in charge, having authority, holding a position or title and having direct reports. However, is leadership really about being in charge of something or someone? Is the definition of a leader one who is in the room, at the table and has a loud voice? Are true leaders those that focus on their power, ego or control over others or are leaders those than can cultivate those entrusted to their stewardship?

In reality, leadership is much more than simply wielding power, position or title. Being a leader is a heavy responsibility that is not for the faint of heart. The adage of 'to whom much is given much is required' (2) is more applicable today than ever. In today's world, leadership is a very risky proposition. In healthcare, for example, this industry has experienced the highest top leadership turnover rates for nearly the last decade than seen in the last several decades or if ever (3).

As leadership circles across various industries are being disrupted, this evolving environment begs several considerations. Why do some leaders fail while others succeed? Why do some leaders make it to the leadership stage earlier than others? Why do some leaders have more success than others? Why are some leaders successful for a long term, while others are just 'a flash in the pan' so to speak?

Today's market is redefining leadership as we know it. From a distance, leadership looks really appealing. Large salaries, fancy offices, travel budgets, influence, power and the like contribute to the allure of the coveted leadership title. However, without outcomes leaders may never make to the stage or hold onto it very long.

In layman's terms, a leader is simply one who has followers. Moreover, the simplest test of one who espouses to be a leader is their ability to influence others without force. Simply put, leadership is the ability to get others to do what you want without force. The reality is that many try, but not all succeed.

Since the definition of leadership is clear cut, why do so many current and aspiring leaders struggle to find the right path? One often overlooked attribute of leadership is time. Leaders are never developed overnight. It takes years of learning, mentoring, testing, trials and pressure to learn the craft and be an effective leader.

The unfortunate reality is that patience is a virtue for some and pitfall for others. Simply put, some aspiring leaders don't want to wait for the stage. They often and irresponsibly run onto the stage before they are ready. An experienced and well-respected thought leader said it best, 'They may run up here, but they will limp back.' In naivety, some leaders or those aspiring view leadership as the pot of gold at the end of the rainbow when, in reality, it's a mirage for those not prepared.

7.1.2 The Fork in the Road

As noted in Figure 7.1, the leadership journey has forks in the road at various stages of the process. Leadership is a process that evolves over time. Leadership has at minimum three phases. Phase 1 relates to those early careerists.

These novice leaders go through phases of educating, learning, training and applying what was learned. Here, early careerists gain basic leadership skills and learn valuable lessons through trial and error. The adage of the 'school of hard knocks' may apply here. Often, this phase includes minimal wins and as many or more failures.

Once base training is complete, early careerists graduate. The graduation test is the fork in the road as noted in Figure 7.1. Option 1 is for

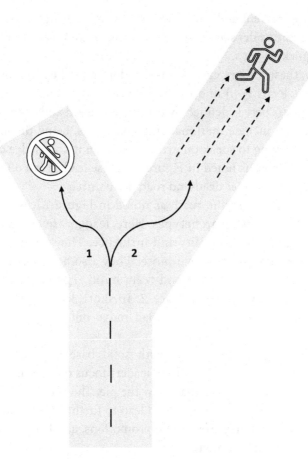

FIGURE 7.1
The leadership fork in the road.

leaders to take the path on the left. As noted, this path is short and fraught with caution. When leaders fail the test, they find themselves focusing on self-ambition, self-interests, pride and the like. Commonly, these naive leaders emulate the 'I' or 'me' mentality. In reality, these leaders simply lack confidence in themselves and their abilities.

Simply put, leaders on track 1 fall to pride, ego, self-interest and a self-centered perspective. The main goal is to gain attention from superiors at all costs in hopes of promotion and further career advancement. They often mimic a chameleon. As a chameleon changes colors to blend into the current environment, so do these leadership archetypes. Their personas change for the current audience and it's hard for outsiders to identify or connect with the leader's 'true self.' Thus, trust becomes an issue and success fades quickly.

Moreover, these leaders may also try to dominate the room or conversations. Their focus is to find one's leadership voice and magnify their presence. Success here is defined by being seen, heard and acknowledged. Common tactics include marginalizing colleagues, being the loudest in the room and trying to speak on every topic even if knowledge or expertise is lacking. Thus, as noted in Figure 7.1, these leaders fall off the stage quickly and hit the career dead-end road prematurely.

Track 2 at the fork in the road, as noted in Figure 7.1, is associated with authentic leadership archetypes. Here, leaders are mature enough to handle success, responsibility and influence. They often only speak when necessary and listen much more. They also have a canny knack to grow the pie, elevate others and team build. The adage of servant leadership definitely applies to track 2. In short, leaders that pass the leadership test at the fork in the road move onto the mid-careerist phase.

Mid-careerist leaders are those with solid base knowledge, education and proven skill sets. Here, these leaders focus on maximizing their knowledge to drive outcomes that grow the pie. The end goal is to establish, cultivate and grow teams that will lead to further synergistic effects. As synergy and outcomes grow, so do promotions, accolades and vertical opportunities for career growth.

Again, the gate to the next career phase is another fork in the road. If these leaders allow success to lead to pride, ego and a self-interested persona, then track 1 will be the road ahead with a dead-end fast approaching. If the leaders prove that they can be trusted with much, then they will find track 2 and move to the next leadership career phase.

The third career phase is synonymous with late careerist. Here, these leaders are very experienced, accomplished and shift their focus to legacy building. Late careerists tend to invest their decade-long career experiences (in most cases) to impact the body of knowledge, share their best practices and cultivate the next crop of leaders to take their mantle or stage. Again, leaders here also are tested along the journey with the fork in the road.

As previously noted, the fork in the road becomes prevalent and leaders either fall off the path or sail smoothing. It all depends on how they handle success. Those that choose self-interests over growing the pie are quickly routed to track 1 and the leadership dead end. In contrast, servant-focused leaders that choose wisely find track 2 and sustained success that stands the test of time.

The takeaway is that leadership is a journey. Leadership takes time, and the journey is fraught many forks in the road. Wise leaders focused on using their gifts, talents and knowledge to help others will find the smooth path. In contrast, their self-interested counterparts will find the dead-end road and a premature end to the leadership journey.

Let's take a closer look on a couple of leadership examples that illustrate these points.

7.1.3 Case in Point

A thought leader was charged with mentoring two up-and-coming leaders. Both were similar in age, education and desire for career growth. However, they were on two different career tracks. The first leader began the career journey with technical skills. This leader performed well as an early careerist, but struggled to find their leadership voice and seat in the room. As time passed, the leader mastered their respective craft and was limited in operational and performance improvement skills. They simply stuck to their bread-and-butter skill set.

As time passed, the leader desired higher levels of responsibility and the associated accolades. A door to the leadership stage cracked open and the leader ran onto the stage prematurely. The leader's persona changed radically overnight. They began to dominate each meeting and perceived success to being the loudest in the room. Also, the focus shifted away from team to 'I' and 'me.'

In short order, the leader became a chameleon. Other leaders and subordinates struggled to relate to the leader's true identity. Trust was lost and the leader began to repel others. Think of shark repellant in shark-infested waters. The louder the leader spoke and more dominant the persona became, the more others distanced themselves from the leader.

The result was that the leaders quickly found themselves at the fork in the road. Track 1 was unknowingly the path of choice. The road quickly came to a screeching halt and dead end. The leader ultimately stifled their growth and career path due to focusing on self-interests versus growing the pie.

The thought leader then compared this journey to the other mentee leader. This leader began with a technical skill set. As time passed, they continued to retrain and educate on the journey. They learned and cultivated both operational and performance improvement skills. The leader also achieved significant outcomes in various operational arenas.

As successes were realized, the leader faced the fork in the road several times. Each time, the leader unknowingly chose track 2 as noted in Figure 7.1. The secret to success was simple. When the fork in the road appeared, the leader looked for opportunities to help others solve problems. The end result was that this leader mastered team building, problem solving and the motto of 'we' or 'us' instead of 'I' or 'me.' Track 2 leads to many vertical career opportunities and associated accolades. Fortunately, this leader avoided pride, ego, and self-interests. Thus, success and leadership tenure grew with time.

7.1.4 Summary

So, what was learned from the previous dialogue? First, leadership is not the act of possessing a title or being in charge of people. True leaders are those that can influence others to do what they want without force. The ultimate sign of success for leadership is the ability to develop teams, build synergy and achieve outcomes that last long term.

Second, leadership takes time. Unfortunately, time requires leaders to exercise patience. For some, patience is a virtue, and for others, it's a stumbling block. With time, leaders learn basic skills, acquire knowledge and build foundations. These fundamentals are building blocks that ensure that leaders can handle the weight of the stage once they arrive. Without a foundation, leaders that run onto the stage prematurely will limp back sooner than desired.

Finally, the biggest leadership test is success. How one handles success will determine if the leader hits a dead-end road prematurely or continues the journey and leaves a noticeable impact on the industry. The kryptonite for leadership is pride, ego and self-interests. Regardless of skill, tenure or career phase, leaders must always focus on 'us' or 'we' instead of 'I' or 'me.'

The reality is that leadership is a risky business. The journey is fraught with many tests (i.e., forks in the road) along the way. Effective leaders are those that choose wisely, grow the pie for others and sail smoothly through the forks in the road. Their counterparts that fall to self-ambition will unfortunately find the dead-end road and fall off the leadership journey prematurely. The key to success is continuously sharing your gifting with others instead of holding on to tightly.

REFERENCES

1. Merriam-Webster, 2021
2. Luke 12:48, NIV
3. American College of Healthcare Executives (ACHE), '*Hospital CEO Turnover Rates Show Small Decrease.*' 2020

8

The Power of Knowledge in Team Success

8.1 THE ULTIMATE TEST OF TEAM SUCCESS

8.1.1 Success Defined

Success can be defined as 'The correct or desired result of an attempt' (1). This concept is synonymous with winning, achieving a goal, a desired end, gaining recognition and the like. However, in reality, is true success really tied to an accolade, title or achieving a tollgate? Is there more to success than just goal attainment? Can success be multidimensional with various degrees of achievement or is it a one-size-fits-all concept? Is success time- and people dependent? Will true success be tested over time by sustainability? Do leaders need a good process to achieve and sustain success for a long term? Will team structure or lack thereof determine the degree of success attained? Is success a high-risk proposition for leaders and organizations to plan for carefully? Can everyone handle success or is the coveted prize better suited for some as compared to others? We will answer these and more considerations in the following.

In simplest of terms, a team is a group of people that come together to achieve a desired end (2). There are a few team archetypes worth noting. First, teams are often structured for long-term collaboration. These may be departments or programs that work together to help the organization achieve its long-term mission. Long-term teams tend to be more formal, traditional and well structured (organization dependent).

DOI: 10.4324/9781003316251-8

Second, teams may be formed for short-term ventures. These teams tend to be heavily goal oriented and focused. The end goal for this team archetype is to achieve its desired end or goal sooner than later. Once achieved, the team may dissolve or only collaborate as the need arises with time.

A good example could be a capital approval team for a service organization. A multidisciplinary team of leaders comes together as needed to approve or deny large dollar capital expenditures (typically tens of thousands of dollars or millions). The goal is to ensure that the organization is viable for a long term. Here, the team's collaboration is cyclical or chronic, but the time invested is limited to each cycle.

The third team archetype worth noting is ad hoc. Here, organizations assemble teams for a specific purpose as the need arises. Typically, the need for collaboration is emergency or critical in nature. A command center in a health system fighting the COVID-19 pandemic is a good example. A team of leaders and stakeholders may assemble for a few weeks to address the effects of a short COVID-19 surge. Once the surge dissipates, the team fades back into their normal roles. The ad hoc team may often be associated with crisis negotiators that collaborate quickly to solve important issues even quicker.

Team success is also multidimensional. Success can be tagged to individuals, a group of people (i.e., the team), a division or the organization as a whole. Also, team success has an impact consideration. Some success may only impact those internal organizational stakeholders such as leaders or staff.

In contrast, some successes may have an external impact to customers, partners, potential partners and the like. Think of a health system that adds several urgent care clinics in a specific region. This would be a win for the organization, its internal stakeholders and the communities served. Customers would have greater access to more affordable and convenient health services when needed. Also, this growth would increase revenue and employment opportunities. In the end, all stakeholders would benefit.

Team success also has a time component. Successes can be short term, mid-range and long term. Short-term team success is typically associated with sustaining outcomes less than a year. Mid-range success can be tied to outcomes sustained one to three years. The ideal success is long term where team success is sustained longer than three years. Here, the return on investment of achieving the success tends to yield the highest gain.

8.1.2 Team Success Tiers

Along with impact and time, team's success can be measured on a tiered structure. See Figure 8.1 for details.

The first tier of team success is team harmony. Here, teams are assembled and begin the journey toward the desired end. Team harmony is achieved when a group of people agrees to work together to achieve a common goal or, in some instances, multiple goals. The adage of 'singing from the same sheet of music' applies here. As the team works together, a cohesiveness is developed where mutual respect and desire to achieve a larger purpose become the main focal points. A simple rule of thumb is for the team to communicate, talk together, laugh together, in some instances cry together and essentially stick together through the best and worst of times.

Second, team success transitions to a synergistic focus. Synergy is 'The increased effectiveness that results when two or more people or businesses work together' (1). Here, individual goals and desires are sacrificed for the team's success. The end goal is to accomplish more together than individually. The focus shifts from 'I' or 'me' to 'we.' With time, trust and success, synergy is grown and maximized.

FIGURE 8.1
Team success tier structure.

The third tier of team success relates to initial successes or wins. Here, the team's cohesive nature and unified efforts drive initial outcomes. These successes or wins may be goal attainment tied to service, cost or quality, for example. Irrespective of the foci, the initial successes are the fuel that keep the engine running. Each initial success provides incentive and motivation for the team to stay the course and keep working together. Moreover, these milestones are validation that synergy is present and the team is functioning as intended. The adage of 'crawling before walking' applies here.

The fourth tier of team success is focused on consistent wins. Is the team able to consistently meet goals or achieve targeted ends? Can the team shift focus on priorities and address issues or targets that were not on the original radar? Typically, well-organized and cohesive teams that are agile can pivot quickly and still achieve intended goals that fall into this category.

A good example here is a team that sets several goals around improving value to thousands of customers. The targeted ends would be to achieve base goals tied to customer satisfaction and quality of services rendered. Then, the team would target stretch goals for each metric once base goals were achieved. The achievement of stretch goals is evidence of the team's maturity, cohesiveness and ability to consistently pivot and realize wins.

The next tier of team success focuses on knowledge transfer. Knowledge transfer in this sense simply pertains to growing the pie and developing the team. Once the team achieves wins that are significant, are the lessons learned being shared throughout the organization or beyond so others can learn from the journey? Does the team have depth in roles in case key members of the team are promoted or transition away from the organization? Is a succession plan present to ensure continuity of services or functions if team members change roles? In short, the key for knowledge transfer is for the organization to ensure that its teams are developed over time and share knowledge so the delivery model perpetuates success versus dying on the vine (operationally speaking).

The final team's success tier relates to sustaining success for long term. If the team succeeds in reaching the desired end or goals, are the gains maintained over time? Are the teams 'one hit wonders' on the national best practice list or do they mature into regular contributors of expert industry knowledge? Can the team handle success and continue to grow, mature and develop talent to ensure that the cycle continues? Or does the team become self-centered, ego-driven and self-absorbed? The key here is whether or not success erodes or strengthens the team's bond, cohesiveness and future journey.

8.1.3 The Process

Team success is also predicated on a good process. See Figure 8.2 for details.

First, leaders must begin with a gap analysis when team building. There are several common considerations worth noting. Does the team have a defined structured? Are roles and responsibilities clearly defined for the team? Is the team equipped with the knowledge and experience needed to

FIGURE 8.2
Team success process.

succeed? Are desired values and norms present or do they need to be cultivated? Is the vision or end goal for team's success well defined? Are the right stakeholders involved in the team-building process to ensure that the desired end is achieved?

Once leaders identify both actual and perceived gaps, the team should conduct brainstorming sessions. The goal is to identify solutions for each gap. The concept of a think tank may be a good fit. Here, everyone is allowed to think outside the box with no constraints and offer insights of what is needed for team success and gap resolution.

Next, leaders should begin planning to make the solutions a reality. The key for successful planning is to ensure that resourcing exists to help the team meet its goals. The premise is simple: identify gaps, set goals to fill the gaps, budget to ensure that resources are present to meet goals and achieve the expected end. If outcomes don't match the desired end, then leaders should revisit the gap analysis, goal setting process and resourcing.

The next phase of the team success process relates to implementation. Here, leaders implement the plans or proposed solutions and remeasure to ensure that the end justifies the means. If any shortfalls in goal attainment appear, leaders should pivot quickly and redirect activities and resources to achieve goals. Once goals are attained and the team succeeds, the organization should celebrate those wins. Team celebration can take many forms including, but not limited to: recognition at meetings, training opportunities, stretch assignments, publications, presenting at industry national venues and the like.

The key is that successful teams have a good process, plan ahead, execute flawlessly, pivot when needed and recognize excellence at every turn.

8.2 CASE IN POINT

Let's look at a couple of examples of how two teams and their leaders missed the mark.

8.2.1 Sports Example

Recently, a renowned college football team in the most competitive market for the venue was restructured. A new head coach arrived and began the team-building process. Thus, a new coaching team was assembled. Next, the new team of coaches began recruiting new talent (i.e., players or team members) with the end goal of winning a national title the same year. In addition to adding new talent at all levels, new playbooks and schemes were introduced with the intent of providing a competitive advantage over competing teams in the conference.

With time, the team was assembled, harmony was established and the team won several games against notable opponents. As more games were played, the team beat more higher ranked opponents and subsequently won the national title the same year. With the added notoriety, came great levels of disfunction. Several key players on the team were Heisman Trophy nominees and began to look for professional opportunities to play football at the next level. The focus shifted from the team to individual accolades and successes. After the winning season, several key players left the team and knowledge gaps were exposed.

Once again, the team was restructured and new talent was drafted in to replace the knowledge that left. The team's performance was grossly different. The team began to lose games to less-ranked opponents. The playbooks were no longer effective and the team lost over half the games each year for consecutive years. Shortly after, the coaching team was transitioned out of the university and the leaders began the rebuilding process all over.

So, what was learned? The team was able to achieve harmony, synergy and initial wins. See Figure 8.2. However, the team was not able to win for consecutive seasons as the wins resulted in a degradation of team cohesiveness. Thus, success was limited to one year and knowledge transfer never occurred. The term 'one hit wonder' became a reality as the team's success was both a blessing and hindrance.

8.2.2 Service Industry Example

A large service industry organization experienced several years of operational declines that impacted tens of thousands of customers annually. These challenges were not sustainable and a change in course was warranted. Senior leaders assembled a small, but very affective, team to conduct an organizational turnaround. The team comprised of very dedicated, knowledgeable and tenured leaders. However, the team members all came from different backgrounds, had not worked together previously and were very different in many ways.

The team came together and centered efforts on saving the organization. The team puts the organization's viability first and synergistic efforts soon followed. The team achieved synergy by creating space for the members to talk together daily, laugh together, eat together and even cry together during tough times. The key to success was allowing each team member to focus on their strengths. This covered the weaknesses of the group and produced best in-class outcomes.

Against all odds, the odd pairings worked. The team began to experience historical success and took the organization from the brink of crisis to being a national leader in the respective field. Goal attainment increased for several years and the team achieved progressively better outcomes even in the face of industry challenges. The team quickly became a national best practice knowledge bearer sharing insights and lessons learned from the wins over a several-year period.

Referring back to Figure 8.2, the team quickly moved up to the fifth tier of team success and maintained that progress over time. As the years passed, the team members began to handle success differently. Most of the team handled it well and kept moving forward. Unfortunately, a few members began to focus on self-interests, promotion, individual accolades, ego and other unfavorable attributes. Thus, tier 6 on Figure 8.2 was never sustained. The team began lane jumping into other member areas of responsibility and infighting which eroded the synergy and cohesive nature of the group. Also, trust became an issue for the first time, and the gains achieved over the years were quickly jeopardized.

8.2.3 Summary

What was learned from both examples and the previous discussion? First, perception is not always reality. Similarly, what sparkles does not always shine. Success is a risky proposition. It has been often said, 'Leadership without succession is failure.' In layman's terms, success is predicated on the ability to plan ahead to ensure that wins of yesteryears are sustained and repeated in the future. If not, success is only a mirage instead of a stark reality.

Second, team success is not determined by meeting one goal or milestone. Success is multidimensional with various degrees or tiers of achievement. As noted in Figure 8.2, ideally successful teams achieve harmony, synergy, cyclical wins, transfer knowledge and sustain success for long term. A lack to achieve all attributes and sustain them is simply marginal or limited success at best.

Finally, the reality is that success is time- and people dependent. Time is a great litmus test of team success. It differentiates 'one hit wonders' from genuinely successful teams. The true test of team success is the ability to achieve the desired ends and sustain those wins over the long run.

The reality is that people ultimately determine how successful teams and organizations are over time. People are the bearers of organizational culture and knowledge which predicate success or failure. Consequently, if teams remain mission focused and avoid self-interests, the journey can be very promising. Unfortunately, not everyone can handle success. Thus, success is more of burden than coveted prize.

Effective leaders are those that can assemble effective teams, achieve success in the long term, grow the pie, share knowledge, think ahead and pivot as needed. Their counterparts will fall short and fail the ultimate test of team success.

REFERENCES

1. Merriam-Webster, 2021
2. Wikipedia, 2021
3. IISE, Lean Green Belt. 2016

9

The Power of Knowledge in Selecting Solution Partners

9.1 LEVERAGING SOLUTION PARTNERS IN HIGH-RISK CHANGE ENVIRONMENTS

9.1.1 Introduction

In today's market, change is the new norm and only constant. As change grows, so does the associated risk. Change occurs when something is made different (1). There are several types of change. Some changes are normal or to be expected. Other changes can be classified as unexpected, disruptive or transformational.

Irrespective of type, the expectation is that everything changes in some way with time. Change denotes and requires a time component. An example of normal change, for example, is aging. The unfortunate reality is that everyone ages over time. This type of change tends to be slow and more controlled which allows people to adjust with time. Thus, it is less disruptive and less risky.

In contrast, disruptive and transformational change happens quickly and tends to be of higher risk. For example, when COVID-19 arrived in the US, there was little fore warning. It essentially changed every aspect of life overnight. These disruptions include, but are not limited to: travel, entertainment, supply chains, financial markets, the provision of healthcare services and many other attributes too numerous to mention. The pandemic was disruptive and transformed everyday life regardless of geographic region, socioeconomic status or industry. This aggressive nature occurred quickly, left minimal room for error and has lasted longer than most expected. Thus, it is of higher risk and more impactful.

One positive aspect of transformational change is that leaders tend to lean heavily on solution partners to weather the storm(s). A solution partner is exactly what the term implies. It is someone who assists leaders in finding answers to problems by providing a skill set, support and insight. However, solutions are not always as readily available or easy as leaders would prefer.

9.1.2 Solution Levels

Generally speaking, there are essentially four levels of solutions worth noting. See Figure 9.1 for details.

The next level of solutions relates to divisional. Here, divisional leaders need assistance with issues that affect a subgroup of departments and/or large divisions of an organization. The key is that the risk, scope

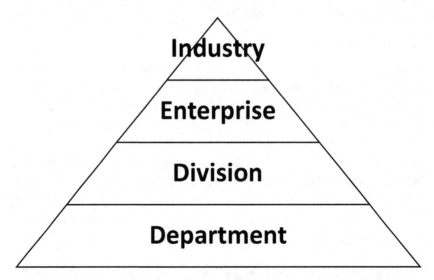

FIGURE 9.1

The first level relates to departmental solutions. Here, leaders are focused on a finite issue or number of issues that impact a department or relatively small group of people (organization dependent). A good example could be productivity rates for a department of healthcare billers. The leader may need help understanding and addressing variation in productivity rates for billers that process over 100,000 bills per year. The nonproductive billers require overtime support from the highly productive billers which costs the organization tens of thousands of dollars per year in unwarranted overtime.

and complexity increase as the number of stakeholders grows. A simple example could be excessive staff turnover rates in 50% of the departments of one division for a large service organization. The high turnover areas have turnover 20% above average as compared to peer departments. This revolving door results in $3 million per year in unwarranted overtime and contract labor expenditures which could be avoided if the turnover rates are reduced by 10% for the division.

The third-level solution pertains to the enterprise as a whole. Here, enterprise's top leaders need assistance with global issues affecting the entire enterprise. Due to the scope and complexity, the risk here is very high. A good example could be a multi-hospital health system that experiences a critical shortage in surgical supplies. Thus, the surgery centers at each facility are forced to reduce cases and, in some instances, close for extended periods of time. The result is a loss of access to life-saving services for many surrounding communities.

The fourth and final solution level applies to a specific industry. Here, industry leaders need solutions for problems plaguing the entire industry across the country. The COVID-19 pandemic is a prime example. One effect of the pandemic in healthcare, for example, is a national staffing crisis for critical workers. As healthcare workers contract COVID-19 and are unavailable to work for extended periods of time, health services are rationed to the most critically ill. The industry as a whole has to collectively work together to ensure that patients in various geographic regions have access to life-saving services.

9.1.3 Solution Dimensions

Along with levels, solution partners have several dimensions worth noting. See Figure 9.2 for details.

Another solution dimension falls into the technical category as noted in Figure 9.2. Regardless of industry, each business has some technical requirement. In healthcare, for example, this technical bucket may include the clinical arenas where patients receive clinical care. Leaders may need a solution partner to address infection rates, customer satisfaction issues, wait times for clinical procedures and the like.

The third dimension of solutions is attributed to support services. Here, the focus is around those areas that help the business run indirectly. Think of facilities management, quality, accreditation, data and analytics,

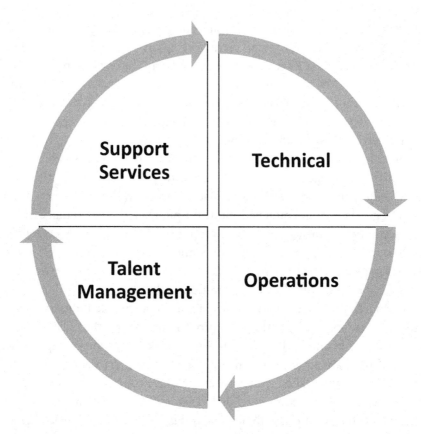

FIGURE 9.2

Solution partner's work typically falls into one of four categories. The first category relates to talent management. As with any organization, people are the most important asset. Here, leaders may need a solution partner to address excessive turnover or vacancies, employee engagement, onboarding of new hires, building trust between staff and leaders and so on.

environmental services and others. The key is that these functions are essential to ensure that the environment, regardless of industry, is safe and effective for the customer base.

The fourth solution dimension relates to the operations arm of the organization. Here, leaders may need help addressing issues around FTE (i.e., full-time equivalent in staffing) approval processes, capital purchases, resource allocation for business units and many others. The focus here is on the operations of the enterprise. Irrespective of foci, operations tend to keep the business running behind the scenes.

In simplicity, partnering for solutions is a relatively simple concept. Right? Unfortunately, that is not always the case. In high-risk environments, leaders and solution partners must choose wisely.

There are a few common considerations worth noting that both parties should answer before agreeing to an engagement. What's the goal of the partnership? What's the probability of success if we partner? Are resources readily available to achieve the goal? Is the goal feasible or simply an unattainable pipe dream? Is leadership open to solutions that will work or will be focused on being comfortable? Is the partnership a good fit for both parties?

If both parties can't agree to the basics, further consideration is warranted. At the end of the day, the purpose is to find solutions to a problem. The solutions will take skill sets, coordination and facilitation. Moreover, as with any change people will have to agree to, support and champion the change for the solutions to stick long term.

However, the million-dollar question is, why do some solution partnerships not succeed? Let's take a closer look at a real-world example.

9.1.4 Case in Point

Recently, a large service organization began training many of its leaders in methodologies such as Lean and Six Sigma. The initial focus was to improve all aspects of the value equation. This relates to service, cost and quality of services provided to many tens of thousands of customers annually. Initially, the enterprise's goal was to create an 'army' of internal process experts to address waste. Think of the eight wastes as taught in Lean courses (2). These wastes may include attributes such as delays, errors, reworks, non-utilized talent and the like.

As time passed, the enterprise shifted its focus to utilize these process experts as change agents. The foci shifted from the eight wastes to a more holistic performance improvement approach. The goal here was to save hard dollars, find efficiencies at every turn, reduce variation in services and enhance the value for each customer across the organization.

The organization pivoted once again and began to view these change agents as solution partners. Often, these leaders would be given stretch assignments in unfamiliar operational areas to help solve issues. The goal was to increase awareness, bring outside perspective to long-standing hard-to-solve issues and achieve breakthrough change. As noted in

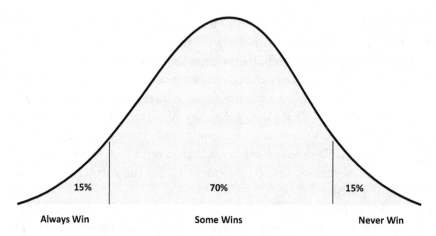

FIGURE 9.3

A thought leader was engaged to assess the process and help top leaders understand why so many solution partnerships were not fruitful. Further analysis revealed some interesting trends. The lagging leaders in the bottom 15% of Figure 9.3 that never won were more persona driven in their partnership selections. Simply put, they favored change agent partners that would support their perspective versus drive transformational outcomes.

Figure 9.3, 70% of the solution partner engagements produced wins some of the time. Fifteen percent of the engagements always produced wins, while the lagging 15% never produced desired outcomes.

There were four questions these leaders used as the litmus test for a good solution partner. First, do we (our team) like the potential solution partner? Second, do they fit in our group's dynamic? Third, will the solution partner support our perception of the problem(s)? Fourth, can we trust the solution partner not to expose our weak points?

In contrast, the thought leader found very different trends with the successful leaders that represented the top 15% of the distribution in Figure 9.3. These leaders objectively vetted their potential solution partners based on several attributes.

- **Has the solution partner achieved significant outcomes in previous engagements?** The fewer the outcomes, the higher the risk. Thus, the less likely the leaders would engage these solution partners for assistance.
- **Does the partner challenge the status quo?** Those partners that challenged the status quo and operating norms were rated as lower risk or

the most viable candidates. Those that were easily swayed by a group majority or favored group think were higher risk and less likely to be selected for an engagement.

- **What is the solution partner's skill set?** Those that possessed a unifocal or bifocal skill set were higher risk and less likely to be selected. Simply put, a unifocal skill set is a partner with only technical skills, while a bifocal skill set involves a partner with technical plus operations skills. The ideal and most often selected solution partners for the top-performing leaders possessed an integrated skill set. Here, the partners had technical and operational leadership and performance improvement skill sets with significant outcomes in all facets. Thus, they were at lower risk and more ideal for the solutions journey.

- **What percentage of wins has the solution partner sustained for long term?** The top-performing leaders more often selected those partners that had a track record of sustaining over 70% of their wins long term. In contrast, those partners that sustained less than 70% of their wins were at higher risk and less likely to be chosen.

- **Has the solution partner been successful in team building?** Those partners that were above average (as compared to peers) in building teams that were cohesive, synergistic, outcomes-driven and sustained wins were at lowest risk and highly prized partners. In contrast, those partners that were below-average team builders were more often not selected by top-performing leaders.

- **Has the solution partner shared knowledge externally?** In short, those partners that were successful in producing sustained wins for long term and published their outcomes were the prime choice of top-performing leaders. Their counterparts that had not published best practices were left in the bullpen for more practice and warmups.

The thought leader also noted a similar trend from the solution partners that were most successful. The partners vetted the potential leaders before selecting assignments. Here, they used a similar screening method for the leaders in need of help.

- **What's the probability of success?** The most successful solution partners selected leaders in need of help that had a track record of successfully solving problems. The leader of choice represented a pull culture where change agents were pulled into the business units and given a blank canvas to diagnose and help solve the issues at hand.

- **Is the issue an organizational priority?** Here, the top-performing solution partners ensured that only issues that were a top priority for leadership were selected. These initiatives tended to have proper executive sponsorship, resourcing and a sense of urgency. Thus, the probability of success was higher as compared to the partnerships that were not on the leadership radar.
- **What's the scope of the issue?** The best performing solution partners tended to select small to moderate engagements that affected divisional- or department-related issues. Those leaders that were more operationally proficient tended to have smaller issues. Thus, the probability of success was higher. In contrast, those leaders constantly involved with 'boil the ocean' issues that were more systemic in nature were at higher risk with a smaller chance of success. In short, the top-performing solution partners chose wisely to ensure that they achieved the biggest bang for their buck (so to speak) by partnering with other top-performing leaders.

9.1.5 Keys to Success

In summary, the lessons learned from the previous dialogue and case study are as follows. First, trust is the most important ingredient to a successful solution partnership. Leaders cannot take a face value approach to trust. Trust does not mean 'we like the partner' or 'the partner will agree with us.' Trust is a mutual concept that involves all stakeholders.

A partnership centered on trust as the foundation encompasses three components: success, excellence and a safe place. Top-performing leaders and solution partners will ensure that everyone contributes to success, everyone focuses on excellence and the team creates a safe place for everyone to succeed and fail. The reality is that everyone is human and often will fail. The test is whether or not the team will recover from failure and try again until success is realized.

Second, successful solution partnerships rely on stakeholders finding the right fit. Here, leaders and solution partners must mutually agree to a predetermined goal that is feasible, customer focused and realistic. The right fit is not persona driven. Leaders must ensure that the solution partner has the skills, ability, proven outcomes, fortitude to challenge the status quo and objective 'street credibility' to successfully lead the change journey. If not, both sides will end the journey with buyers' remorse.

Similarly, the solution partner must vet the leaders in need of help. Here, the key to success is ensuring that the leader in need of help has a track record of success, possesses operational fortitude geared toward high performance, resourcing for the journey is present and the leader has a desire to win. Otherwise, the solution partner is a risky proposition not worth the effort.

Finally, leaders and solution partners must realize that all change involve risk. As change grows, so does the associated risk. Proper alignment between partners, goals and the desired end will ensure that the risks are low and the team has the greatest probability of success.

The key here is measurement. Leaders don't know what they don't measure. Ignorance is never bliss. What leaders and teams don't know will eventually unfavorably impact them, the customer and enterprise as a whole.

Effective leaders are those that understand risk, measure effectively, avoid risky propositions and always land on the safe bet (i.e., the ideal solution partnership).

REFERENCES

1. Merriam-Webster, 2021.
2. IISE, Lean Green Belt, 2016.

10

The Power of Knowledge in Leadership Growth and Development

10.1 PEARLS AND PITFALLS OF LEADERSHIP STRETCH ASSIGNMENTS

10.1.1 Developing Leaders

Leadership development can take on many forms. By definition, leadership development 'is the process which helps expand the capacity of individuals to perform in leadership roles within organizations' (2). Often, organizations develop their leaders with classroom training, advanced degrees, specialty certifications and the like. Other leadership grooming may take a more personal approach where 'up and comer' leaders are paired with more experienced leaders to learn the craft through formal knowledge transfer. This is often referred to as leadership sponsorship programs.

In other instances, leaders are developed in the format of stretch assignments. A stretch assignment is typically an opportunity offered to high performers for advancement purposes. The purpose of this function is both a test and a reward. For those higher performers that can achieve higher-level outcomes in stressful environments, the reward may be promotion, financial incentives and the like. In contrast, for those leaders administering these pressure tests, it provides an opportunity to test the talent pool so the 'cream will rise to the top' so to speak.

These opportunities may take the form of assignments to new projects, learning new tasks or skills beyond a leader's current role (1). Irrespectively, stretch assignments by name alone connote a dyad relationship between positive gain and painful stimuli. Think of an athlete that stretches before the Olympic trials. The stretch may provide some level of relief or satisfaction if controlled within certain pain tolerances. Contrarily, if the athletes stretch their muscles too far, then pain and often injury may result.

The same premise applies to leaders. In some instances, leaders seek next-level opportunities for a variety of reasons. Exposure or visibility to work on important projects that garner the attention of senior leaders is one driver of accepting a stretch assignment. If all goes well with the project, this opportunity could be a trampoline to catapult the candidate into a higher and more prestigious role. However, if the assignment does not go as expected, it could be a career ender just as fast.

Another driver of leadership pursuits for stretch assignments may be learning, growth, resume building and skill mastery. It depends on the current state of the leader. However, working on unfamiliar projects with others outside of the business unit often proves to provide invaluable learning and growth potential. Again, the key is to ensure that the project or task achieves the desired end. Otherwise, the end result may be a tarnished reputation or impediment to future opportunities.

Leaders also seek out these pressure tests with the end goal of increasing their promotability potential. The key here is to look forward. The focus tends to be long term or down the road. There are a few considerations worth noting.

What skill sets will the organization need in the next one to five years? Are there any organizational gaps currently in those skill sets? If gaps exist, then stretch assignments may be a good launching pad for leaders to position themselves properly to fill organizational talent needs. Thus, promotion potential will grow.

A final consideration for leaders pursuing stretch assignments may be financial gain. Again, it depends on the assignment, organizational need and resourcing. However, financial incentives may take the form of higher salaries during or after the assignment. Also, promotions for those successful higher performers may increase the leader's earning potential (both current and in the future).

Although stretch assignments may add value and produce career pearls, there is a flip side to the process. Often, leaders seek out next-level opportunities with little to no forethought. Think of a race car driver. They are all suited up in the driver's seat of a race car, the car is running and their foot is on the accelerator. However, they don't know which direction leads to the racetrack, finish line and subsequent winner's circle. As a result, when the race starts they barrel full steam ahead in the wrong direction. They not only lose the race but lose prize money, endorsements and future career opportunities in the process.

Leadership is very similar. Leaders that haphazardly race into stretch assignments may often get more than they bargained for on many fronts. As with the race car drivers, the leaders race into a fire that they are not equipped to extinguish or take on assignments that are extremely high risk with little chance of success. Thus, in the end, they are left with buyer's remorse (so to speak) instead of a launching pad for success.

10.1.2 Practical Examples of Pitfalls

Over the years, myself and other colleagues have witnessed this firsthand with many leaders. Some are successful with these pressure tests, while others are not. The real question is why? Let's take a closer look at a couple of real examples for more insight.

In conversation, a thought leader shared their experience as an early careerist. The leader was a top performer and 'up and comer' so to speak. The organization of the time began Lean Six Sigma training and senior leadership hand selected a dozen or so mid-level (director or divisional leader level) top-performing leaders as candidates for this inaugural cohort. The premise was simple. Offer the cohort prime education and training. Select the top performers for stretch assignments. Then, create a senior leader talent pipeline from the cohort to craft the next generation leadership team that would guide the organization for decades to come.

The cohort of leaders was overly eager for this assignment. All leaders 'raced' into the training not knowing what it entailed. Fortunately, all the candidates were able to pass the basic course qualifications. Postgraduation, less than 10% of the cohort was successful in the long term with the skill set.

In short, the majority of leaders produced little to no return on investment (ROI) from the training related to cost savings or performance improvements. Only one or two leaders excelled with the added knowledge and leveraged it as a catapult for next-level opportunities. Thus, both the organization and most of the cohort leadership participants lost out on what could have been a pearl. Unfortunately, the stretch assignment quickly turned into a pitfall experience for most.

Another example relates to a mid-careerist whose ambition or desire for next-level roles outpaced their ability to produce relevant cross-functional outcomes. This leader worked for years in their industry and acquired respectable amounts of formal education. To say the least, they were respected as a quasi-expert in their field. Over the years, the leader was viewed as a backbone or crucial piece of the organizational portfolio related to the respective business unit.

As the organization's leadership changed, a gap surfaced in another business unit. The leader was offered another assignment to lead the business unit during transition in addition to their normal duties. This stretch assignment required the leader to essentially perform two full-time leadership roles at once with the latter assignment being outside of the leader's comfort zone. There was no formal goal other than making it through a period of time until another leader was identified for the vacant role. The arrangement was very informal and no guarantees or financial incentives were offered for the additional duties.

The leader was again like the race car driver. They barreled full steam ahead into the assignment without much forethought. The idea of being included in executive leadership circles with greater organizational exposure was overwhelming enticing and alluring. As time passed, the leader found themselves overwhelmed and working an unsustainable schedule.

The new workdays extended to 14- to 16-hour days. This trend spilled over into the weekends. The leader sacrificed a lot of time personally to fulfill this assignment. In short, the leader quickly ran into buyer's remorse and realized that the end most definitely did not justify the means. The distraction of the stretch assignment resulted in retrenchment of the home business unit's performance. Thus, the expected gain of outcomes turned into a dual operational loss for both business units.

So, looking back at these two examples, it's imperative to examine the situation from a different lens. The key question to answer is, what was missing? In short, there are two simple tools leaders can use to assess their stretch assignment opportunities to ensure that they find the pearl instead of stepping into a pitfall. Let's take a closer look.

The first tool worth noting is a decision tree as noted in Figure 10.1. Leaders must consider several attributes of stretch assignments before taking the plunge. The first question to ask is if the assignment has a well-defined goal. The goal is also synonymous with desired end. Goals should be specific and measurable. These attributes ensure that leaders are headed in the right direction, achieve the desired end and can measure progress or lack thereof along the journey. If a stretch assignment does not have a defined goal, leaders should reconsider the opportunity as noted in Figure 10.1.

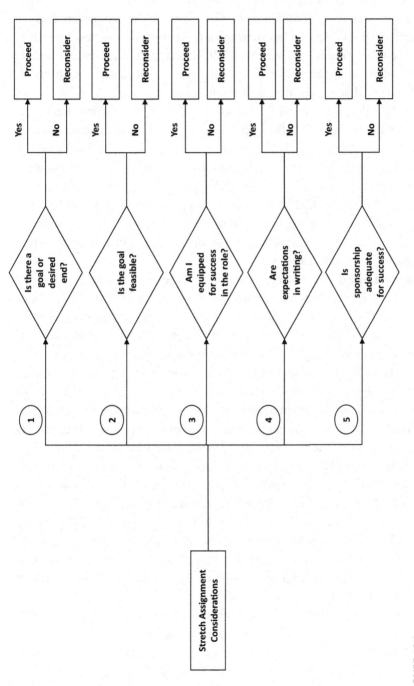

FIGURE 10.1
Stretch assignment decision tree.

The second question leaders must consider before agreeing to a stretch assignment relates to goal feasibility. Is the goal for the assignment feasible or realistic? This helps leaders determine their chance of success for failure before committing to a new responsibility. As noted in the figure, leaders should reconsider the opportunity if the goal is not realistic. Otherwise, the leader will be set up for failure from the start.

Third, leaders must consider a healthy dose of self-reflection. Do I have the attributes to be successful with this stretch assignment? Attributes may include knowledge, skill, abilities, political capital and cultural influence. In short, leaders must ensure that the opportunity fits with their capabilities. If not, then they should reconsider the assignment and look for a better fit.

Fourth, leaders should have expectations placed in writing. As with the first thought leader example related to Lean Six Sigma training. Nothing was in writing. The leaders jumped headfirst into the training and verbal promise of promotion after success.

However, the organization failed to formalize these promises which left some of the leaders looking for their next role without support from leadership. The key here is for leaders to ensure that any agreements between themselves and the organization for the stretch assignment are detailed in writing before accepting the responsibilities. These topics may include explicitly outlining compensation during and after the stretch, promotions, next-level opportunities and the like. The worst case scenario is for leaders to succeed in the pressure test, but not get rewarded as promised. If written verification of expectations and promises is missing, leaders should reconsider the opportunity by looking for a better fit.

Finally, leaders must consider sponsorship. Successful and sustainable change requires a good sponsor. A sponsor typically takes the form of a senior leader who is skilled, knowledgeable and possesses political capital to achieve cross-functional success. If any of these attributes is missing, the leader should look for a better opportunity. Otherwise, accepting the stretch would be the equivalent of being 'thrown to the wolves' operationally speaking. Without adequate sponsorship, aspiring leaders would, more than likely, face a non-value add experience.

The second tool leaders should consider before committing to a stretch assignment is a risk assessment as noted in Figure 10.2. Figure 10.2 outlines the five attributes noted in the decision tree: goal, goal feasibility, leadership abilities, sponsorship and written expectations. As noted, leaders can list each stretch assignment.

Stretch Assignments	Is There a Goal? 1- Yes 2-No	Is the Goal Feasible? 1- Yes 2-No	Am I Equipped for Success? 1- Yes 2-No	Is Sponsorship Present? 1- Yes 2-No	Are Expectations Written? 1- Yes 2-No	Risk Score *Sum Columns 2-6 Lower Score = Lower Risk	Risk Level	Action Plan
Opportunity 1	1	1	1	1	1	5	Low Risk	Prime Opportunity
Opportunity 2	2	2	2	2	2	10	High Risk	Seek Other Options
Opportunity 3	1	2	1	2	1	7	Low Risk	Prime Opportunity
Opportunity 4	1	2	2	1	2	8	Average	Proceed with Caution
Opportunity 5	2	2	2	2	1	9	High Risk	Seek Other Options
Avg Score	1.4	1.8	1.6	1.6	1.4			
Risk Level	Low Risk	Low Risk	Low Risk	Low Risk	Low Risk			

FIGURE 10.2

Once listed, each opportunity is ranked on each of the five attributes. The goal is to identify low-risk stretches versus those that pose a higher risk to the accepting leader. Let's take a practical view of Figure 10.2. The first opportunity is low risk. Here, the leader is facing an assignment that has a well-defined and feasible goal, adequate sponsorship, written expectations of compensation and is a good fit for their respective skill set. Thus, this stretch is a prime opportunity for the leader and would produce the greatest amount of value.

In contrast, opportunity 2 in the figure is of high risk. Here, the stretch assignment does not have any of the five required elements as previously noted. Thus, it is of high risk and the leader should consider other opportunities. Otherwise, the leader may be faced with an impossible situation or dead-end road.

Opportunity 4 in Figure 10.2 is a unique situation that poses average risk to the leader. This stretch assignment has a well-defined goal. However, the goal is risky in that its feasibility is questionable. Also, the opportunity is not the best fit for the leader's skill set and no written expectations are readily available. However, the stretch does have a good sponsor to help with success. The key here is for the leader to proceed with caution and accept this offer as a last-case scenario if no other low-risk options are available.

10.1.3 Summary

So, what did we learn from the simple analysis of stretch assignments? First, anytime leaders consider stepping out of their comfort zone and taking on additional responsibilities, there are risks and rewards. The goal is to maximize rewards and minimize leadership risks. Second, what sparkles does not always shine. Leaders don't know what they don't measure. The old adage of 'measure twice, cut once' applies here. Leaders must measure risk levels before jumping headfirst into stretch assignments. Third, simple risk tools are essential for leaders to position themselves for greatest success.

As one's career progresses, the reality is that time is finite. Once a day is gone, we can't get it back. As is written in Ephesians (5:16 NIV), we must make the most of every opportunity. It's imperative for leaders to engage in next-level opportunities that add value. Value can manifest in the form of extra compensation, promotion, resume building, learning, relationship development and exposure to new opportunities just to name a few.

The key for leaders to find those pearls and avoid the pitfalls is understanding risk. Ignorance is never bliss. What leaders don't know can and will have negative consequences in the long run. Accepting a high-risk stretch assignment without forethought is the equivalent of picking up a snake before one knows if it is venomous or not. Low-risk stretches are those that pose the lowest risk to the leader's success potential and should be viewed as prime opportunities. In contrast, high-risk stretch assignments are a signal for leaders to pursue other growth options that add greater value.

Effective leaders are those that use their time wisely, choose low-risk pearl assignments, avoid high-risk pitfalls and measure their success along the way. Only those that understand, mitigate and minimize risk will succeed in the long term.

REFERENCES

1. Forbes,'4 Rules for Accepting a Stretch Assignment,' 2019. Jo Miller. *www.forbes. com/sites/jomiller/2019/02/14/4-rules-for-accepting-a-stretch-assignment/?sh=4d35 cf09566b*
2. Wikipedia, 2021. *https://en.wikipedia.org/wiki/Leadership_development*

10.2 PEARLS AND PITFALLS OF ENGAGING IN LEADERSHIP COACHING

10.2.1 Organizational Knowledge

Organizational knowledge is one of the hottest topics in today's market. Many strategists and thought leaders use various terms to describe this concept. Common synonyms may include, but not be limited to:

knowledge transfer, knowledge sharing and the like. However, is organizational knowledge accurately captured in these tag lines? The short answer is not entirely.

Knowledge can be defined as 'information, understanding, or skill that you get from experience or education' (1). It is synonymous with knowing, learning, education, training and development. In simplest terms, organizational knowledge is simply the knowledge that an organization possesses to meet and exceed customer requirements. There are four main components of organizational knowledge worth noting.

The first is people. All knowledge begins and ends with people. Since people make up organizations and determine how work gets done, they tend to be the most valuable knowledge source particularly in service industries. One of the most common knowledge transfer foci is succession planning. Although it's a good starting point, leaders can be deceived quickly if this topic creates tunnel vision. Simply put, organizational knowledge far extends the boundaries of a succession plan.

The second component relates to training and investment. One often overlooked aspect of investing in people is time. It simply takes time to develop talent. Time is finite and very expensive. Once a day is gone, we don't get it back. Thus, leaders must ensure that the knowledge investment in training, grooming and developing organizational talent achieves the desired return on investment. This return may take the form of enhanced revenue, cost savings, higher quality of services, longer tenure and the like. The goal is, for leaders, to invest in people and subsequently have the people use what they have learned to benefit the organization and its customers.

The third aspect of organizational knowledge is culture. In simplest terms, culture is the way work gets done in an organization. It is synonymous with the soul of the organization. Formally, culture is 'a way of thinking, behaving, or working that exists in a place or organization' (1). The best adage used often states, 'leadership sets culture and culture drives quality' of services, outcomes, etc. The reality is that the people in any organization are the knowledge bearers. They also collectively create, sustain and perpetuate the organization's culture. Thus, culture is a prime factor in organizational knowledge.

The last component is outcomes. Does the organization collect, measure, analyze and share data related to outcomes driven by organizational knowledge? Common focus areas may include financials, quality of services, customer feedback or satisfaction and the like just to name a few. A deeper dive of knowledge transfer key performance indicators (KPIs) may include vacancy rates, turnover rates, the percentage of the employee population that can retire within three to five years, the percentage of leadership roles with an identified successor to the current leader and many more. The key here is that leaders must ensure that a talent pipeline is readily available, trained, equipped and customer focused to ensure that organizational outcomes are on target and sustained for long term.

Often leaders focus on a variety of knowledge transfer techniques to ensure that organizational knowledge is present, cultivated and driving desired outcomes. These techniques may include, but not be limited to: succession planning, employee or leader turnover, cross training, executive coaching, investing in a knowledge management system, paired work, e-learning and many others. The goal is to develop, retain and share knowledge across the enterprise and beyond (as appropriate).

10.2.2 The Case for Leadership Coaching

For the sake of this conversation, let's focus on executive or leadership coaching. The concept of coaching is synonymous with lead, guide, mentor, council and shepherd, and shows others a better way of doing something (1). In simplest of terms, leadership coaches provide clarity, guide leaders along the career path and ensure that resources are available to help leaders make critical career decisions. Thus, choosing the right leadership coach is imperative for leaders to succeed in the long term.

There are several reasons leaders may consider a coaching experience. First, leaders may desire promotion opportunities which require additional skill sets that the leader may not possess. It may also be a required element for next-level roles to be organization dependent. The premise is that coaching provides an extra layer of leadership maturity which will benefit the organization and leaders in next-level roles. Thus, coaching may be a required element for promotion to ensure that skills related to influencing others, mastering the art of change management and the like are present.

The second driver for leaders pursuing a coach may be to gain insight. Leaders or their superiors may be interested in the feedback from a 360 review, for example. The key with this exercise is for leaders to receive confidential and blinded feedback related to how peers and colleagues see them or the work they produce. Insight gained from leadership coaching may also include opportunities for the leader to manage change better or communicate more effectively.

In some instances, leaders may use the 360-review process to identify their leadership peer friends, neutrals and foes. Friends are staunch supports. Neutrals typically have a leader's best interest in mind from a distance. In contrast, foes will never support the leader's success. This insight is crucial for leaders to reach optimal success as friends and neutrals will accelerate success, while foes if not mitigated can impede career progress. In short, the coach in this instance provides vital insight into a leader's current portfolio that can be improved upon in hopes of greater career opportunities.

Third, engaging a leadership coach may be a requirement for a leader's employment or next-level role. Some leaders that struggle with outcomes may be assigned a management plan to help turn the corner to better outcomes. Often, leaders may be required in these plans to engage a coach. In most instances, management plans that entail a coaching opportunity many times are a blessing in disguise although the process may be painful at the start.

10.2.3 Coaching Focal Points

Along with leadership coaching drivers, there are three phases of one's career in which coaching may be warranted. The key is for coaching to be tailored to the current career phase. The first career phase is often referred to as early careerist. This refers to leaders in the first decade or so of their careers. Here, leaders are focused on establishing base skills, being promoted, gaining influence with peers and overall leadership development on a basic level.

The next phase relates to mid careerists. Here, leaders have moved beyond the basics of leadership and focus heavily on mastering the skill set or career. These leaders tend to possess basic skills, advanced skills and have produced significant outcomes respected by organizational peers. The focus of leadership coaching in this phase could be preparation for senior-level roles, greater influence or even impacting the industry body of knowledge outside the organization.

The third phase related to sun setters. The most experienced leaders typically in their last decade or so of the career journey are the focus here. Sun-setting leaders may need coaching that focuses on finishing legacy projects, developing aggressive succession plans for their successors or impacting the way industries (plural) do work. The key is that leadership coaching must be tailored to the leader's current need and current career phase. Otherwise, the experience may quickly become a non-value add experience.

10.2.4 The Ideal Coach

The most important decision leaders will make when considering a coaching experience is selecting the right coach. The ideal leadership coach should possess several basic characteristics. First, a good coach should have respectable industry experience and significant outcomes as a leader. Insight, empathy and a 'bird's-eye view' are required for coaches to successfully guide leaders in the right direction. Without experience, coaches will simply be theorists instead of insightful guides to the leadership promised land. Furthermore, the simplest test of a leadership coach's metal is the outcomes attained as a leader, in operations or leadership roles. If outcomes are missing, leaders should keep looking for the ideal coach.

The ideal coach should also have an independent or unbiased perspective. The end goal is for the leader to improve. If a leadership coach is biased in any way, the leader may be steered in an unhealthy direction that leads to buyer's remorse. Thus, the ideal coach must be independent or neutral in their perspectives and guidance.

Finally, a good leadership coach should be resourceful and goal oriented. Does the coach offer a coaching timeline with tollgates? Does the coach set measurable and specific goals with the leader from the start? Does the coach offer templates, source material for theories and data during the coaching sessions? If not, leaders should keep looking for the ideal coach.

10.2.5 Coaching Selection Tools

In pursuit of the ideal coach, leaders may be interested in a few tools that include a coaching timeline, decision tree and risk assessment tool. The coaching timeline can be summarized in Figure 10.3.

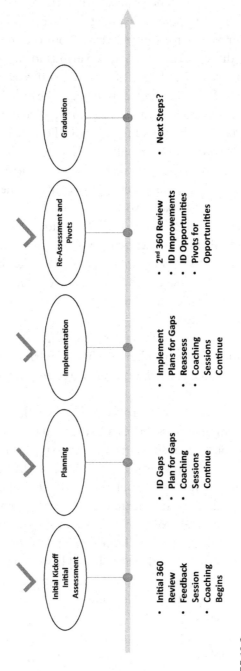

FIGURE 10.3
Coaching roadmap timeline.

A good coaching experience starts with a kickoff meeting between the coach and leader. It's important to note that the coaching roadmap should be mutually agreed upon by both parties from the start of the coaching journey. Also, these journeys may take various forms or direction based on the goals, desire end and need of each respective leader.

The purpose of this initial contact is to begin the initial assessment. Here, the coach and leader start with a meet and greet session that quickly evolves into formal dialogue. The initial focus is for the coach to gain insight via conducting a 360-review assessment on the leader and have the leader complete a personality assessment in most cases. Once these data and information are readily available, the leadership coaching journey really begins.

Next, the leader and coach work as a team to identify strengths and gaps in the leader's performance from the information gained from the 360-review and other assessments. Plan development quickly follows for concrete actions, goals, desired tollgates and the like that the leader will focus on in weeks to come. During this phase, coaching sessions continue and the two stakeholders work together to find solutions for identified improvements as needed.

The third phase of the coaching timeline as noted in Figure 10.3 relates to implementation. Here, the plans are fully implemented. Along the way, data are collected to ensure that progress is being made. The coach and leader may choose to informally engage peers and other stakeholders independently for feedback as to improvements or lack thereof from the leader.

Next, the coaching process moves into the final leg. The coach and leader may choose various reassessment techniques to measure progress. It is reasonable for a second 360 review to be completed as a comparison to the first assessment. The goal is to test the plan to ensure that the leader is improving, achieving goals along the journey and headed to the desired end.

Finally, the leader and coach must agree on a graduation timeline. This all depends upon the progress with the plan and tollgate achievement. The key for this tool is that a good coach should have a timeline, help create a vision for the coaching journey and resource the leader appropriately so all goals are attained. If this tool is missing, leaders should reconsider the coaching opportunity.

Another tool for leaders to identify the ideal coach is Figure 10.4. A decision tree is a simple tool where the leader needing guidance assesses the coach before agreeing to the journey. Here, the leader should answer several questions. Does the coach have the experience and significant

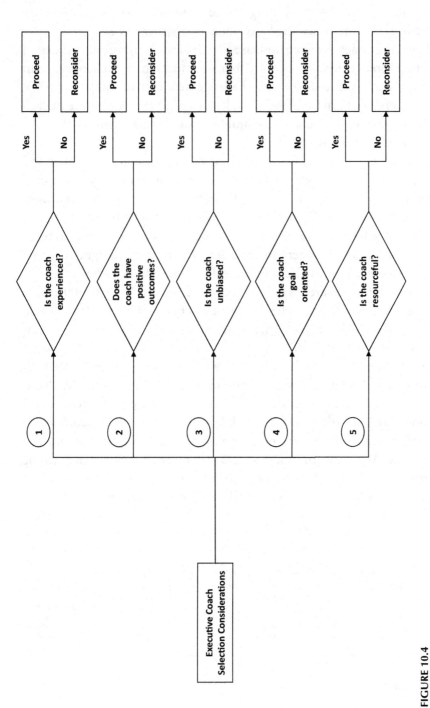

FIGURE 10.4
Decision tree.

outcomes in leadership, coaching and/or operations to guide the journey effectively? If not, the leader should look for another coach.

Does the coach have an unbiased perspective? This really relates to internal versus external coaches. Often, organizations may choose to train internal leaders as coaches. The challenge here is that organization history and politics can interfere. Thus, leaders must ensure that their coach is independently and objectively guiding the process. If not, the leader should look for another guide.

Finally, the leader must determine if the coach is goal oriented and resourceful. As noted previously, an ideal coach is an expert in their own right that couples experience, insight and theory to guide leaders. Does the coach have a wealth of resources (i.e., templates, literature reviews) and goals for the leader's journey? If not, further consideration is warranted.

The final tool for leaders to consider in selecting the right coaching experience is a risk assessment. In reality, leadership coaches can be at high risk in various arenas for the leader's career. As noted in Figure 10.5, the same five coach attributes, as noted in Figure 10.4, are risk assessed. The lower the risk to the leader, the better. As noted, there are five potential coaches in consideration.

As an example, the first coach is at low risk as they are experienced with outcomes, unbiased, goal oriented and resourceful. Thus, the leader would view this coaching experience as a prime opportunity. The second coach option is at high risk. Here, the coach lacks experience and outcomes, and doesn't have a solid plan with measurable goals and lacks resources to guide the leader. As a result, the leader should seek other options from a coaching perspective. The fourth coach, for a different comparison, is at average risk. Here, the coach is goal oriented with good experience, but lacks an unbiased

Executive Coaches	Is the coach experienced? 1- Yes 2-No	Is the coach unbiased? 1- Yes 2-No	Does the coach have positive outcomes? 1- Yes 2-No	Is the coach goal oriented? 1- Yes 2-No	Is the coach resourceful? 1- Yes 2-No	Risk Score *Sum Columns 2-6 Lower Score = Lower Risk	Risk Level	Action Plan
Coach 1	1	1	1	1	1	5	Low Risk	Prime Opportunity
Coach 2	2	2	2	2	2	10	High Risk	Seek Other Options
Coach 3	1	2	1	2	1	7	Low Risk	Prime Opportunity
Coach 4	1	2	2	1	2	8	Average	Proceed with Caution
Coach 5	2	2	2	2	1	9	High Risk	Seek Other Options
Avg Score	1.4	1.8	1.6	1.6	1.4			
Risk Level	Low Risk	Low Risk	Low Risk	Low Risk	Low Risk			

FIGURE 10.5
Summary.

approach, resources and significant outcomes as a coach or leader. Thus, the leader should proceed with caution in accepting this coach for the journey.

So, what did we learn from the previous dialogue? First, organizational knowledge is the key for success. People and the knowledge they possess or lack will directly impact the longevity and survivability of the enterprise. Second, leaders seek coaching for a variety of reasons. In some instances, leadership coaching is optional, while, in others, it is mandatory for the current or next-level role. Also, leaders may seek a coach for assistance with a promotion or gaining insight as to who their friends, neutral or foes are professionally speaking.

Third, coaching must be tailored to the career season of each respective leader. As noted, there are three basic career phases. Those early in their careers may need help with basic skills while those mid to late careerists will focus heavily on mastering the career journey and impacting others outside the organization. Here, change management, leadership influence, communication and other notable skills tend to garner much of the foci. Thus, the coaching plan must be tailored specifically to each leader's respective needs and current career phase.

Finally, leaders must choose their guides along the career journey wisely. Not all leadership coaches are created equally. Leaders must ensure that their guides have the experience, outcomes, resources, direction and unbiased perceptive. If all these attributes are present, the coach is likely to be a pearl or value add experience. If any are lacking, the leader may easily step into a career pothole unknowingly and miss the desired promised land.

The key takeaway is that selecting a leadership coach is a risky proposition. However, how will leaders choose wisely if they don't know the risk? The short answer is they won't. Leaders must always revert to the basics such as measurement and comparative analysis when making critical career decisions. Leaders don't know what they don't measure and ignorance is never bliss.

Effective leaders are those who use objective measurement to identify career guides that add value at each turn in the career path. Moreover, and more importantly, these leaders master the art of identifying, mitigating and avoiding high-risk pitfall coaches who are ill prepared to objectively guide them to the career promised land.

REFERENCE

1. Merriam-Webster, 2021.

11

The Power of Knowledge in Measuring Success

11.1 PEARLS AND PITFALLS OF VALIDATING IMPROVEMENTS

One of the biggest challenges for leaders is to determine if improvement is really real or just a mirage. Per *Merriam-Webster*, an improvement is 'the act or process of making something better.' The concept of improving is synonymous with enhancement, advancement or refinement (1). In layman's terms, an improvement is simply a change from the old in a positive direction.

Often leaders desire to improve for a variety of reasons. These desires are commonly referred to as drivers of change. Common targets for improvements may include: improve revenue, reduce costs, improve quality of services and enhance customer satisfaction or value. The end goal from this perspective is to improve value to the organization, its people and the customer. Value is essentially anything a customer is willing to pay for (2). These drivers tend to be common across all industries and the traditional focal points of improvement efforts.

Improvement can also be viewed from a similar but different lens. Leaders may seek to improve and validate the results for a promotion or next-level role opportunity. This accomplishment may be used as a differentiator between themselves and peers who are competing for the same next-level roles. Improvement may also be a required job function and included in the leader's annual goal expectations. For example, the leader may be required to improve sales by 10% from the previous year in order to receive additional financial incentives or retain their role.

Similarly, leaders may desire improvement to prove or disprove models and concepts. In many thought leadership circles, designing new ways of doing business and proving the models or concepts will work cross functionally is a prized skill set. However, a model or a concept without validated improvement is just a theory and not worth its weight until proven effective. Leaders may also want to improve something to gain greater visibility for themselves or their teams. This visibility may add credibility to their work and provide greater opportunities to impact the industry body of knowledge.

There are several considerations leaders must entertain when determining if something has improved. One of the biggest missteps leaders often make is assuming that couple data points moving in the right direction is an improvement. Is this actually an improvement? The short answer is not always as two data points never make a trend.

To adequately validate an improvement, leaders must first begin with data. The key is to gather data both before and after the change. The amount of data needed can vary based on the topic, how it is measured, the frequency of measurement and the like. The key is to have enough data that adequately represent the topic of focus. For example, if the leader's aim is to improve quality scores (i.e., infection rates) for a hospital by 20% in the next 12 months and only monthly data are available, then it would be acceptable to compare 12 months of infection data before and after the change. Ideally, leaders would want to analyze at least 20 data points for the KPI (key performance indicator) in question.

Once representative data are available, there are three simple questions to ask.

1. Is the KPI meeting goal?
2. Is the KPI improving to achieve goal?
3. Are the KPI's data in or out of control?

The goal here is to avoid data analysis paralysis. I equate this to my early days as a paramedic. We worked for a very busy hospital-based 911-system ambulance service and treated thousands of cardiac patients per year. These cases ranged from simple heart issues to life-threatening heart attacks.

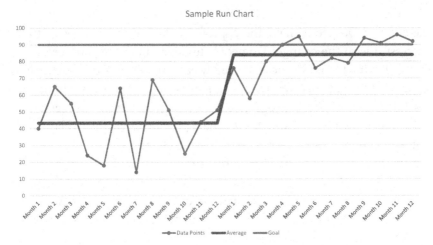

FIGURE 11.1

The run chart is simply a line graph. The keys here are to have at least 20 data points if possible at minimum. Also, the chart should display the goal over time. It's also reasonable to use an average line for the data points in various time series as noted in Figure 11.1.

The tool of choice for diagnosis in the field at that time was an EKG. Medics learned to read these EKGs and became so proficient that they could diagnose a heart attack or lack thereof in a matter of seconds by using this tool and answering a few simple questions. They didn't have to over analyze data and other test results to determine if someone was having a life-threatening emergency. Moreover, the EKG was a very valid and reliable diagnostic tool.

The same premise applies here. Leaders should simply place the data in a run chart to start. See Figure 11.1 for an example.

As shown in Figure 11.1, there are 24 data points represented by month. This essentially outlines 12 months before and after the change. The goal for the figure is 90 and the ideal direction is higher is better. As noted, the KPI data are not meeting goal on average. However, the data are trending toward the goal post improvement. After the change, the KPI data increased and headed in the desired direction.

So, what does this tell us? Simply put, there was some level of improvement post change. The data are headed in the right direction and further consideration is warranted to exceed the goal. In this scenario, the leader would need to reassess people, structure and process to reach the breakthrough outcomes that would consistently meet or exceed the goal.

Simple considerations are as follows: Are the right people involved in the change? Do people have the appropriate knowledge and skills to be successful with the change? Do people understand the new process? Are they following the new process correctly each and every time? Is the right structure in place to ensure that people following the process will be successful? Is the right technology available to support the new process, etc.?

The takeaway is that a simple run chart provides a visual display of the improvement or lack thereof as a starter consideration.

Next, the question at hand is to determine if the data are in or out of control. A simple control chart can be used for visual display of the same data. As noted in Figure 11.2, the data are out of control. This is evidenced by a shift (i.e., six or more consecutive data points above the average line) upward in data points 15–24.

As a side note, there are many scenarios that could present here. One would need further training on statistical process control (SPC) and the western electric rules (2) for insight. However, for the purpose of this review, the data are signaling a change in direction has occurred. This simply means that the improvement efforts have directed outcomes in the desired direction. Thus, the leader's efforts should be to continue heading

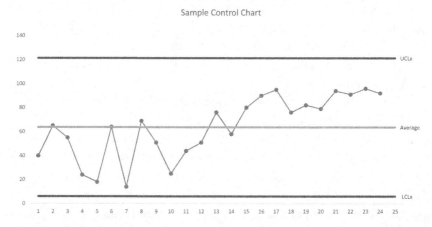

FIGURE 11.2
Once the run charts and control charts are assembled and analyzed, leaders may want to consider testing the data further for significance. Here, the goal would be to test the data before and after improvement or to change to ensure that it is significant at the 95% confidence level or higher. Leaders would need to rely on change agents (i.e., black belts) to help with these calculations. However, the added insight and data validation would provide further credibility of the improvement and outcomes.

in the same direction with desired pivots to meet and exceed the expected goal as previously noted.

11.1.1 Pitfalls to Avoid

As leaders assess their data and validate improvement efforts, there are several pitfalls to avoid. First is the lack of visual display. Again, it's imperative to stress the use of a simple run chart at minimum to display data over time. If the data are not improving to goal over time, then leaders will know at a glance from viewing the chart that the improvement efforts need to be adjusted.

Second, avoid the two-data-point perception. Many times, over the last couple of decades, colleagues and myself constantly hear leaders saying, 'We have improved "x" as evidenced by two months of improved performance.' This is considering that the KPI was measured in months. Thus, two data points were the focal points.

Often, over time, the perceived improvements were proved to be random variation and performance trends either declined or did not improve to goal as expected. The takeaway is that perception was not reality. The premise is simple. Avoid the two-data-point perception by using ideally 20 or more data points over time (if possible) visually displayed in a run chart at minimum.

The third pitfall to avoid is not testing data post improvement for significance. Presuming that improvement in averages is real improvement can be misleading in certain circumstances. Thus, leaders should consider using other techniques such as test of hypothesis and the like. If black belts or other data-oriented skill sets exist in the organization, leaders should leverage them to ensure that the perceived improvements were significant.

The final pitfall is data analysis paralysis. When validating improvement efforts, leaders should keep it simple. The best analysis is one that is clear, concise and to the point. Ideally, leaders just need to answer a few questions quickly:

- Are the data meeting goal?
- Are the data improving to achieve goal?
- Are the data in or out of control?
- Are the data post improvement significant?

Answering these basic questions will ensure that leadership perceptions of improvement are reality. Without this consideration, the adage of 'being a hero in your own mind' takes on greater significance.

11.1.2 Summary

As noted, improvement can take on many forms. Improvements can be perceived, reality, temporary, long term, or hidden based on the initiative and how data are displayed. The key is that leaders don't know what they don't measure. Often, perception is not reality and further consideration is warranted.

When validating improvements, leaders should follow a few simple steps. First, set a realistic and measurable goal. Second, measure outcomes over time and frequently. Third, visually display the data in a simple run chart at minimum. Fourth, validate that the performance trend is moving toward the goal at minimum. If not, pivot quickly to redirect outcomes. Finally, understand and prove that a perceived improvement is actually real.

Leaders will be most effective by leveraging simple tools such as run charts and control charts to identify, verify and magnify their improvement pearls. In contrast, leaders should avoid the pitfalls of not visually displaying data (i.e., improvements), focusing on a few data points and not validating perceived improvements. The key is simplicity, clarity and knowing fact from fiction.

REFERENCES

1. Merriam-Webster. 2021
2. IISE, Lean Green Belt. 2016

Conclusion

Knowledge is a powerful tool that determines whether organizations and their leaders succeed or fail with strategy, planning, governance, team building, and decision making.

Organizational knowledge is synonymous with knowledge transfer, knowledge sharing, and the like. The concept involves people and requires some form of action. Knowledge will not voluntarily transfer itself between people groups. Leaders and their organizations must harness, control, and leverage the power of knowledge to achieve goals, grow the pie for others to win, and ensure that they are 'in the know.'

As noted, all knowledge is not the same. Ignorance is never bliss. What leaders and their organizations don't know will eventually impact them and their customers unfavorably. The key to organizational knowledge is measurement. Measuring knowledge takes many forms. Measurement tools range from simple gap analysis to advanced risk assessments. However, the underlying current is that organizational knowledge will determine whether or not an organization succeeds in the long term. A lack of knowledge can prevent leaders and organizations from reaching their full potential and fulfilling their mission.

The reality is simple. Knowledge matters. It's an essential component for leaders, their teams, and organizations to succeed in the long term. What we don't know can and will be a problem at some point along the career journey. The more we know, the better off we are. Thus, leaders and their organizations must realize, value, and leverage the power of organizational knowledge. Otherwise, they will simply die on the vine (operationally speaking) due to a lack of knowing, insight, and forethought.

Index

Note: Page numbers in *italics* indicate a figure on the corresponding page.

Other Books by This Author

The Ideal Performance Improvement Eco System
Quick Guide to Improvement Made Easy

The Ride of a Lifetime
Seeing the Impossible Become Reality
A Local Public Servant Rises from Obscurity to the World Stage

The ABC's of Designing Performance Improvement Programs
What Thought Leaders Must Know to Succeed

Conquering the Giants
A Quick Guide for Leaders to Win the Battles &
The Wars Along the Career Journey
Pearls of Wisdom that Academics Don't Teach

The 10 Cardinal Sins of Leadership
What Thought Leaders Must Never Do to Succeed in
High-Risk Environments

Fit for the Fight
17 Keys Leaders Need to Win Big in High-Risk Environments

The Mystery of Leadership
Unlocking the Code to Value, Risk & Leadership Illusions

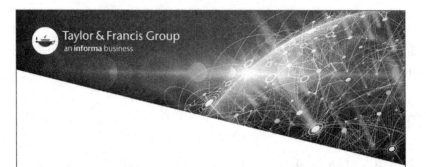